"Any reasonable, sentient person who looks at Spain, comes to Spain, eats in Spain, drinks in Spain, they're going to fall in love."

ANTHONY BOURDAIN, CHEF & TRAVEL WRITER

LIST OF CONTENTS

INTRODUCTION

If you've bought this book, you're obviously interested in buying a home in Spain. You aren't alone – around 63,000 foreigners purchase a property every year, and account for 12-14% of the market. With a year-round warm climate, excellent communications, a healthy lifestyle, wallet-friendly cost of living and a wide range of properties to suit all tastes and budgets, it's easy to see why Spain is so popular.

However, buying property in Spain involves a procedure and regulations that are likely to be different from those in your home country. You may be familiar with some, but you're unlikely to be au fait with everything.

That's where **The Guide to Buying Property in Spain** comes in.

This book includes just about everything you need to know about the property purchase, from the initial stages when your dream is just taking shape, right through to getting the keys to your new front door.

It will help you pinpoint locations that are right for you and decide which type of property to buy. It gives you information on property prices, the people you need to help you and the costs involved in a purchase. It also details the purchase process and provides information about owning a home.

But perhaps most of all, this book will open your eyes wide to buying a home in Spain.

A property purchase, whatever the price, is always a major financial investment and never something to be entered into lightly. This book will help you know what to expect and, more importantly, how to avoid problems.

Ultimately, I hope it gives you the tools you need to make the right decisions so that you can buy a dream home rather than a nightmare. I look forward to hearing how your experience goes – buying a home in Spain allows you to enjoy a fabulous lifestyle in one of Europe's most beautiful and welcoming countries. And in the sunshine!

¡Bienvenidos a España!

Joanna Styles

Important Note

Joanna Styles and the Guide to Malaga team have done their best to ensure the information contained in **The Guide to Buying a Home in Spain** is correct and up-to-date.

However, you should note that laws and regulations for property purchase in Spain aren't the same as those in your home country and are liable to change.

This book is no substitute for professional advice from an expert and you should always take independent legal advice before you pay any money or sign any documents.

Joanna Styles and Guide to Malaga accept no responsibility for any loss, inconvenience or injury that may arise to anyone due to the information included herein.

WHY BUY A PROPERTY IN SPAIN?

What's inside this chapter

- The benefits of buying a home in Spain
- Things to think about before you buy

WHY BUY A PROPERTY IN SPAIN

Buying property in Spain isn't just a financial commitment; it's a decision that can affect your lifestyle, your family and your future. It, therefore, needs careful consideration and thorough research. And all this before you even start browsing property portals! This ebook has been written to help you with the process.

To start the ball rolling, let's spend a little time looking at why you might want to buy in Spain.

The benefits

Spain tops the rankings for the world's favourite property destination for many reasons. They include:

- Guaranteed sunshine and warm temperatures for most of the year (up to 320 sunny days on the Costa del Sol, for example).

- Easy to travel to and from most large European cities at any time of year, particularly if you choose the Costa del Sol, Costa Blanca or the Canary Islands.

- Value for money property in most areas.

- Good potential for rental returns, especially in coastal areas.

- Relatively low cost of living, especially when it comes to food, drink and entertainment.

- Healthy and high-quality lifestyle.

- Welcoming and friendly locals.

- Well-established foreign communities in many parts of the Mediterranean coast and on the islands.

TOP TIP

As with all life-changing decisions, weigh up your pros and cons carefully, do meticulous research and take professional legal advice.

Things to bear in mind

Nowhere is perfect and Spain is no exception. Bear in mind the following:

- High costs associated with buying (at least 8% of the purchase price and up to 13% in some areas – see page 96.

- Pitfalls and problems with the legal side of a property purchase if you don't use an independent specialist lawyer.

- Unexpected renovation and/or refurbishment costs, particularly if you buy an older property.

- Potentially stiff competition for rental clients in the most popular resorts, especially for holiday lets.

- Relatively high taxes on owning a property and rental income for non-residents.

- Overcrowding during the high season in many coastal areas and on all the islands.

Holiday home or second home

This is the main reason for buying in Spain for most people. A property on the Spanish coast or islands will provide you and your family with a great place for holidays for years to come. If this is the main motivation behind your purchase, consider how much you will use the property each year and then, calculate all the running costs.

Permanent home

You might be planning to take the plunge and relocate to Spain to work or retire. If you plan to work, research areas carefully for employment possibilities. If you're retiring to Spain, look at areas with the right amenities and leisure activities nearby.

Planning to move to Spain? Then you need our relocation e-guides to the **Costa del Sol** and the Costa Blanca. **Get 50% off list price with the code WEB** – just add at the checkout guidetomalaga.com/shop.

Buy-to-let

If you're buying to rent out your property (long-term or for holidays), there are different considerations such as:

- Whether your income (rent) will cover all running costs.
- How much competition is in the same area.
- The length of the holiday season in your chosen location.

DID YOU KNOW?

To work out gross rental yields from a buy-to-let, calculate the annual rent as a percentage of the purchase value before expenses. Typical gross yields in Spain range from 5 to 10% a year.

WHERE TO BUY A PROPERTY IN SPAIN?

What's inside this chapter

- Location, location, location...
- All the factors you need to think about when deciding where to buy.

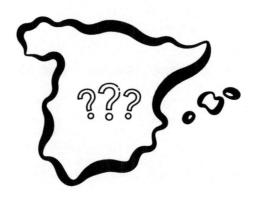

Where to buy?

Location, location and location are famously the three most important criteria when buying property. And together with price, it is usually the other deciding factor. After all, a dream home in the wrong place can easily become a nightmare. So, to help you choose the right location for your property in Spain, we've listed some important things to bear in mind.

We've also included area guides to give you a snapshot of the most popular places in Spain with foreign property buyers. Each description includes a general overview and facts on population, airports and property prices. We've also added a short list of pros and cons for each area. But bear in mind that these are personal - what we see as benefits could well be drawbacks for you. And vice versa!

The population figures for our area guides are for 2020 and come from the Spanish Institute of Statistics (INE). Note that for some coastal areas such as the Costa Brava, we've included the provincial population. Property prices are based on asking prices published on the Idealista property portal in mid-November 2021.

Who are you buying for?

If you're buying the property for your holiday home or permanent home, your needs and preferences take priority. On the other hand, if you're buying to let, the requirements of prospective tenants or holidaymakers should be your first concern.

For example, you may not mind a 2-hour journey to the airport, but holidaymakers generally don't want to travel more than an hour to their rental. You might relish the idea of living in an area with a large expat population, but a family on holiday could be looking for a more Spanish experience.

The weather

Spain enjoys the most sunshine hours in Europe, making the climate its top attraction. The Mediterranean coastline enjoys between 300 and 325 days of sun a year and the Canary Islands have almost year-round sunshine – not for nothing are they known as the 'land of the eternal spring'!

Spain is a big country, surrounded by the Atlantic Ocean and Mediterranean. It is also very mountainous (peaks over 1,000m high are very common). As a result, weather conditions vary a lot from one region to another and there are also microclimates.

Average daily temperatures

Location	January	April	July	October
Barcelona	13°C	18°C	28°C	21°C
Costa Blanca	12°C	16°C	26°C	20°C
Costa Calida	11°C	15°C	26°C	20°C
Costa de la Luz	13°C	15°C	22°C	19°C
Costa del Sol	12°C	17°C	26°C	20°C
Gran Canaria	22°C	23°C	24°C	25°C
Mallorca	14°C	19°C	29°C	23°C
Madrid	9°C	19°C	31°C	18°C
Santander	10°C	13°C	20°C	17°C

DID YOU KNOW?

There are huge differences in the weather on the coast and just a few kilometres inland where it's generally cooler in the winter and hotter in the summer.

Area guides

Mediterranean

The most popular places to buy property in Spain are almost all on the Mediterranean coast. The year-round pleasant climate and stunning scenery make a winning combination for both tourists and homebuyers, Spanish and other nationalities.

In this section, we look at the seven most popular Mediterranean *costas* with foreign buyers:

North-east coast - Costa Brava and Costa Dorada.
East coast - Costa del Azahar, Costa Blanca and Costa Calida (Costa de Murcia).
South coast - Costa de Almeria and Costa del Sol.

Area guides

Mediterranean - Costa Brava and Costa Dorada

In Catalonia in the north-east of Spain, the Costa Brava and Costa Dorada generally have mild winters and summers, relatively high rainfall and around 2,600 sunshine hours a year.

Costa Brava

Europe's package tourism began in Lloret de Mar in the 1950s and since then, the Costa Brava has welcomed millions of tourists every year. The coastline runs from the French border to Palamós, via a succession of pretty coves and picturesque fishing villages, and then as far as Blanes, with a wider and more developed coastline.

The most popular and developed resorts are Blanes, Lloret de Mar and Tossa de Mar, all in the south, while quieter resorts such as Cadaqués (home to Dalí) and Roses lie in the north. Girona, an attractive medieval city, is the capital of the region and located about an hour's drive inland from the coast.

Population: 782,000
Nearest airports: Girona Airport has a limited choice of flights to Europe, with a much wider selection at Barcelona.
Pros: attractive scenery, some of Spain's quietest coves, easy access to Barcelona.
Cons: very busy in high season, poor connections to more remote parts of the coast.
Property prices: villas and country homes in the quieter resorts in the north fetch a premium, while apartments in the south are generally cheaper.
Average square metre price (November 2021): €2,011

Area guides

Mediterranean - Costa Dorada

Stretching from Castelldefels, south of Barcelona, to the River Ebro delta, the Costa Dorada consists mostly of flat golden sands (hence the name), with the occasional fishing village converted into a holiday resort. Much less developed and with considerably less tourism than the Costa Brava, this coastline is quiet out of season when many places all but close down.

The exceptions to this are the resorts of Salou and Sitges, both attractive and offering good amenities, and Tarragona, the capital of the Costa Dorada. The city has some of Europe's finest Roman monuments.

Population: 817,000
Nearest airports: Barcelona, Spain's second busiest airport, is a major international flight hub.
Pros: excellent sandy beaches, mild winter weather.
Cons: quiet out of season, monotonous landscape.
Property prices: Apart from Sitges where homes tend to be triple the average Costa Dorada price, property is among the cheapest on the Spanish coasts.
Average square metre price (November 2021): €1,389

Area guides

Mediterranean - Costa del Azahar, Costa Blanca and Costa Calida

In the east of Spain, the Costa del Azahar, Costa Blanca and Costa Calida are warmer and drier than Catalonia and enjoy up to 2,850 sunshine hours a year.

Costa del Azahar

Known as the Orange Blossom Coast, this area runs from the River Ebro delta in the north to Valencia in the south. Known for its miles of sandy beaches, vast orange groves and marshlands at Albufera, this is one of Spain's quieter coasts. Its main resorts include Benicarló and Peñíscola, the prettiest resort in the far north, and Benicassim and Oropesa del Mar to the north of Castellón, the capital.

Construction is mainly low-key, except for the area around Oropesa, home to Marina d'Or. This purpose-built holiday complex is the poster child for over-development during the last property bubble (2004-7). Even today, many properties remain unsold.

Population: 585,500
Nearest airports: Castellón Airport has a limited number of European flights; Valencia Airport offers a wider choice.
Pros: scenic towns and villages in the north, easy access to Valencia (Spain's third-largest city).
Cons: quiet out of season, limited amenities, over-development around Oropesa.
Property prices: over-supply has kept prices down in the area around Oropesa and Benicassim, while homes are up to 50% more expensive in more sought-after resorts such as Peñíscola.
Average square metre price (November 2021): €1,092

Area guides

Mediterranean - Costa Blanca

One of Spain's most popular holiday spots and a favourite with foreign property buyers, particularly British, many of whom call the area home. It runs for over 100km from Gandia in the north to the Mar Menor in the south. It's known for its vast white beaches (that include dozens with blue-flag status), pretty resorts in the north and pleasant year-round climate.

The north (Gandia to Benidorm) is more mountainous and home to the most attractive resorts such as Jávea and Denia as well as the most development, epitomised in the high-rise blocks in Benidorm and Calpe. Alicante, the capital, is a bustling city with good amenities. The south is flatter, drier and hotter, with sprawling resorts such as Torrevieja and Orihuela Costa.

Population: 1.89 million
Nearest airports: Alicante Airport has an excellent choice of direct flights to European cities year-round. Murcia Airport, with a more limited selection, is a good alternative for resorts in the south.
Pros: some of Spain's best beaches, warm year-round climate, good amenities.
Cons: heat and humidity in July and August, packed in high season.
Property prices: one of the Costa Blanca's main attractions for foreign property buyers is its prices, considerably lower than on the Costa del Sol or Mallorca, for example. Homes tend to be cheaper in the south and in resorts more popular with Spanish holidaymakers such as Santa Pola and Villajoyosa. Moraira and Jávea have the most expensive property.
Average square metre price (November 2021): €1,675

Area guides

Mediterranean - Costa Calida

Known as the 'warm coast' and also as the Costa de Murcia, the Costa Calida runs 250km from San Pedro del Pinatar, on the border with the Costa Blanca, to Mazarrón. It includes the Mar Menor, the largest saltwater lake in Europe and currently suffering from heavy contamination. The landscape is generally flat and unattractive, although there are some excellent sandy beaches.

The main resorts include La Manga del Mar Menor, a narrow strip of coastline between the Mar Menor and the Mediterranean, Los Alcázares on the Mar Menor and Puerto de Mazarrón. The coastline includes the historic city of Cartagena that has fine Roman ruins and is a popular cruise destination. Foreign buyers (mostly British) also favour inland towns such as Alhama de Murcia and Torre Pacheco.

Population: 400,000
Nearest airports: Murcia Airport has a limited choice of flights to European cities.
Pros: dry, warm weather year-round, cheap property particularly inland.
Cons: very hot in the summer, monotonous landscape.
Property prices: the Costa Calida offers some of the cheapest on the Spanish coastline. The most expensive homes are located around La Manga, particularly in the vicinity of La Manga Club, while the cheapest are in inland towns and villages.
Average square metre price (November 2021): €1,068

Area guides

Mediterranean - Costa de Almería and Costa del Sol

In Andalusia, in the south of Spain, the Costa de Almería and Costa del Sol are hotter and drier than both Catalonia and Levante and enjoy 3,000 sunshine hours a year.

Costa de Almería

Set on Spain's most south-eastern corner, this coastline runs around 150km from Roquetas del Mar in the west to Vera in the east. It's the driest part of Spain and includes the Tabernas Desert (the only desert in western Europe), the Cabo de Gata natural park and rugged mountain ranges.

The main city is Almeria and the most popular resorts are Roquetas del Mar and Aguadulce to the west of Almeria. Around the corner going east is Mojácar, a pretty white town, followed by a succession of small towns such as Cuevas del Almanzora, Vera and Huércal-Overa, all popular with British property owners.

Population: around 500,000
Nearest airports: Almeria with a limited choice of direct flights to European cities.
Pros: year-round warm and dry weather, cheaper property than other popular *costas*.
Cons: a slightly remote location, very hot inland in the summer.
Property prices: generally much cheaper than the Costa del Sol or Costa Blanca, although you pay a premium in places such as Mojácar and San José (Cabo de Gata). It's still possible to pick up a real bargain inland.
Average square metre price (November 2021): €1,088

Area guides

Mediterranean - Costa del Sol

One of Europe's most popular holiday destinations with around 13 million tourists a year, the Costa del Sol is also a well-established favourite with foreign residents. It stretches 175km from Sotogrande in the west to Nerja in the east and is developed along almost the entire coast. Amenities are excellent and available year-round and the Costa del Sol has some of Spain's best sports facilities including world-class golf courses.

The scenery is dramatic with high mountain ranges close to the coastline almost everywhere. Its capital is Malaga (Spain's sixth-largest city) and its biggest resort, Marbella. Other popular places to buy property include Manilva, Estepona, Mijas Costa, Fuengirola, Benalmadena and Torremolinos to the west of Malaga and Torre del Mar, Torrox Costa and Nerja to the east. Inland, the Costa del Sol is dotted with pretty white villages such as Casares, Mijas and Cómpeta.

Population: 1.4 million
Nearest airports: Malaga (wide choice of direct flights to European cities) and Gibraltar (UK flights only).
Pros: year-round warm climate, excellent communications, amenities and sporting facilities, well-established foreign population.
Cons: very busy in high season, high humidity in the summer, expensive property in many resorts.
Property prices: one of the most expensive places in Spain to buy property, especially at the west end around Sotogrande, Marbella, Estepona and Benahavís. Homes are generally cheaper inland and in eastern resorts such as Torre del Mar.
Average square metre price (November 2021): €2,442

Area Guides

Atlantic - Costa Verde and Costa de la Luz

The Costa Verde runs along the entire north coast of Spain and takes in the regions of Galicia, Asturias, Cantabria and the Basque Country. They tend to have mild wet winters and enjoy around 1,800 sunshine hours a year.

At the other end of the country, in the south-west, is the Costa de la Luz in the region of Andalusia. It has mild winters and around 2,800 sunshine hours a year. The weather here is generally windier and wetter than the next-door Costa del Sol.

Area Guides

Atlantic - Galicia

Galicia sits on Spain's north-western corner and has its wildest and wettest weather. It's known for its centre of Christian pilgrimage (at Santiago de Compostela), stunning beaches, Celtic roots and delicious seafood. Galicia rarely features on foreign property buyers' radar but those that buy tend to choose the Pontevedra coast around Arousa.

Population: 2.7 million
Nearest airports: Santiago Airport has limited flights to Europe in the summer and very few in the winter.
Pros: stunning landscape, excellent beaches.
Cons: wet weather year-round, lack of international flights.
Property prices: Galicia has some of Spain's cheapest property and in inland villages, you can pick a real bargain. However, homes in the best beach resorts around Arousa attract a premium.
Average square metre price (November 2021): €1,200

Area Guides

Atlantic - Asturias

Asturias is one of Spain's smallest and greenest regions and has a rugged coastline backed by high mountain ranges in the stunning Picos de Europa, the habitat of bears and wolves. Its main towns are Avilés, Gijón and Oviedo, the region's capital. Small towns and villages (including some of the remotest in the country) dot the rest of the region.

Population: 1 million
Nearest airports: Asturias Airport has very few flights but reasonable domestic connections.
Pros: stunning scenery, friendly locals and an outdoor paradise.
Cons: poor international connections, wet winters.
Property prices: they're at their highest in the main cities, particularly Gijón, and in seaside resorts such as Ribadesella. Inland, village houses sell very cheaply.
Average square metre price (November 2021): €1,334

Area Guides

Atlantic - Cantabria

One of Spain's smallest regions but also one of its most scenic, Cantabria is home to miles of sandy beaches and the stunning Picos de Europa mountain range. It has become more popular with foreign buyers, particularly from France, Belgium and Holland over the last few years, and is a favourite with Spanish holidaymakers from Madrid. The bustling port city of Santander is the region's capital and the main resorts are Comillas and Suances in the west, and Santoña and Laredo in the east.

Population: 580,000
Nearest airports: Santander Airport has a small choice of international flights.
Pros: beautiful coastline and countryside.
Cons: quiet out of season, limited amenities outside Santander.
Property prices: homes in Santander and the most popular resorts such as Comillas are among the most expensive in this part of the Costa Verde but you can still buy village homes cheaply.
Average square metre price (November 2021): €1,482

Area Guides

Atlantic - Basque Country

One of Spain's smallest and richest regions, the Basque Country is known for its spectacular coastline, beautiful cities including Bilbao, San Sebastian and Vitoria and fine dining. The Basques have their own language (*euskera*), culture and a strong independence movement.

Population: 2.19 million
Nearest airports: Bilbao and Vitoria both have airports, with a wider choice of flights from Bilbao.
Pros: excellent communications and amenities, beautiful scenery.
Cons: wet weather for much of the year, expensive cost of living.
Property prices: they reflect the high standard of living and San Sebastian has some of the most expensive property in Spain.
Average square metre price (November 2021): €2,682

Atlantic

Costa de la Luz

Known for its bright light (hence its name), strong easterly winds, excellent seafood and vast sandy beaches, the Costa de la Luz starts in Tarifa, Spain's southern-most tip, and continues west for around 200km to Sanlúcar de Barrameda on the Guadalquivir River. This coast's capital is Cadiz and the main resorts include Tarifa, Zahara de los Atunes, Conil, Chiclana and El Puerto de Santa Maria.

Much of the coast is undeveloped except for the areas surrounding Tarifa, Conil and Chiclana. Most resorts are quiet out of season but packed at Easter and in July and August. Inland are the region's famous white villages such as the stunning Vejer de la Frontera and Medina Sidonia.

Population: around 600,000
Nearest airports: Malaga (numerous direct flights to European cities) and Seville (more limited choice).
Pros: less developed coastline and quiet resorts out of season, some of Spain's best beaches, pleasant weather year-round.
Cons: strong winds all year-round, very busy in high season, poor international connections.
Property prices: in some parts of the Costa de la Luz, e.g. Tarifa and Santi Petri, they're similar to those in Mijas and Benalmadena on the neighbouring Costa del Sol. North of Cadiz, prices tend to be cheaper with properties in Chiclana and Sanlúcar among the cheapest.
Average square metre price (November 2021): €1,555

Balearic Islands

One of Spain's most popular regions with tourists (around 13.6 million visit every year) and also a magnet for foreign property buyers, particularly German and British. The three main islands have very different scenery and atmosphere, but they share the contrast between bustling coastal resorts and quiet inland villages and towns. They generally have mild winters with warm summers and around 2,700 sunshine hours a year. However, conditions are usually windy and torrential rain is common in the autumn.

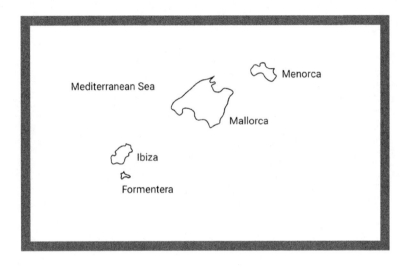

Balearic Islands - Mallorca

The largest and most populated island, Mallorca is dominated by the Sierra de Tramontana mountains in the north-west and flat fertile plains in the south. The capital, Palma de Mallorca, is an attractive city with excellent amenities and home to nearly half the island's residents. Resorts nearby include El Arenal and Magaluf in Palma Bay, both heavily developed and known for their 'lager lout' tourism.

In contrast, much of the island elsewhere is undeveloped or home to quiet resorts in secluded bays or coves. Mallorca also has several stunning towns such as Andratx, Deia, Pollença, Sóller and Valdemosa.

Population: 846,000
Nearest airports: Palma de Mallorca, the third busiest in Spain, with a wide range of flights in high season and fewer in the winter.
Pros: beautiful scenery, good amenities, stunning coastline.
Cons: very busy in high season, over-developed in some parts.
Property prices: Mallorca has some of the most expensive property in Spain, especially in the northwest and north of the island. Villas and traditional country homes (known as *masías*) abound. Holiday lets aren't permitted in some parts of the island.
Average square metre price (November 2021): €3,067

Balearic Islands - Menorca

Flat and green, Menorca has a windswept coastline dotted with dozens of beaches. Much less developed than Mallorca and Ibiza, it has two main towns – Mahón the capital and Ciudadela, both with attractive harbours and fine Georgian buildings. Resort areas include Cale Morell, Fornells and Son Bou where most holiday homes are situated.

Population: 92,400
Nearest airports: Menorca Airport is small and outside high season has flights to mainline Spain only.
Pros: quiet and slow pace of life, attractive scenery.
Cons: poor connections in the winter months, windy year-round, could be too small for some.
Property prices: of the three main Balearic Islands, Menorca has the cheapest homes. The market tends to have a limited selection of properties for sale and there's little new construction.
Average square metre price (November 2021): €2,049

Balearic Islands - Ibiza

The nearest island to the mainland, Ibiza is also considered by many to be the most beautiful. Its rugged coastline is home to fine beaches and stunning coves, often accessible only on foot or by boat, while inland, you'll find rolling hills and olive groves. Known as Europe's party capital, Ibiza is known for its 24-hour dance clubs and relaxed vibe.

Most of the island's residents live in the capital, Ibiza, an attractive city built on a rocky outcrop. Other resorts include San Antonio and Santa Eulalia, both over-developed and popular with 'lager-lout' tourists, while Portinatx and Cala Longa are quieter.

The small island of Formentera (9,150 inhabitants) lies to the south of Ibiza. Mostly barren and with very few amenities, it has little property for sale and few foreigners buy there.

Population: 124,000
Nearest airports: Ibiza Airport has a wide range of flights to European cities in high season but it's limited to domestic connections to Barcelona or Madrid in winter.
Pros: beautiful scenery, stunning beaches.
Cons: very busy in high season, expensive.
Property prices: Ibiza is famed for its secluded millionaire mansions and as a result, has some of the most expensive property in southern Europe. Strict building regulations mean there's little new construction.
Average square metre price (November 2021): €5,026

Canary Islands

Known as the 'fortunate isles', the Canaries sit in the Atlantic off the west coast of Africa and consist of seven main islands, all of which are very different. Tourism is the mainstay of the economy and unlike the rest of Spain, the islands have two high seasons: winter and summer. The main tourist destinations are Gran Canaria, Lanzarote and Tenerife. Between them, they welcome over 15 million visitors a year.

Temperatures on the larger islands (Fuerteventura, Gran Canaria, Lanzarote and Tenerife) range from 20 to 27°C all year round and they bask in 3,000 to 3,400 sunshine hours a year. It rarely rains and some locals don't even own an umbrella!

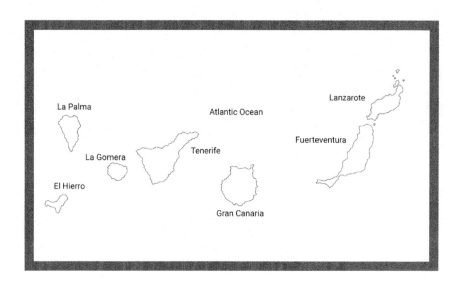

Canary Islands - Fuerteventura

The second-largest island after Tenerife, Fuerteventura is largely flat, windswept and undeveloped. It's also home to some of the best beaches in Spain and is a renowned destination for wind and kite surfing. Puerto del Rosario is its capital and the main resorts are Corralejo in the far north and Costa Calma and Jandía in the south.

Population: 120,000
Nearest airports: Fuerteventura Airport has direct flights to some European cities and a good shuttle service to the other islands including Tenerife (with the biggest choice of flights).
Pros: unspoilt beaches, warm weather year-round.
Cons: windy year-round, limited amenities.
Property prices: they're generally cheaper than Tenerife, although villas in Corralejo and Jandía come at a premium. Apartments are common in resort areas.
Average square metre price (November 2021): €1,246

Canary Islands - Gran Canaria

Home to the islands' capital and one of the largest cruise ports in Europe, Gran Canaria is a land of contrasts. While the south is mostly flat with a vast sandy coastline, the centre and north consist of high peaks, dotted with mountain villages.

The south is home to the most popular holiday resorts and the famous Maspalomas sand dunes. Resorts here include Playa del Inglés, San Agustín and Puerto Rico. Las Palmas city is attractive and lively with a year-round cultural scene.

Population: 855,500
Nearest airports: Las Palmas Airport has a wide range of flights to Europe and mainland Spain year-round.
Pros: warm weather all year, stunning scenery, good amenities.
Cons: densely populated for the size of the island, could be too small for some.
Property prices: generally higher in the southern resorts, particularly for frontline beach properties. Homes tend to be apartments or small detached houses with a maximum of three bedrooms.
Average square metre price (November 2021): €2,034

Canary Islands - Lanzarote

Almost desert-like, Lanzarote is an island of white houses, black volcanic rock and yellow lunar landscapes. It's known for the Timanfaya mountain range, unspoilt beaches (Famara and Costa Papagayo are two of the best) and its legacy from Cesar Manrique, an artist and sculptor. He made the island his home and ensured much of it remained undeveloped.

Arrecife is the capital and the main resorts are located on the south coast. They include the more up-market Playa Blanca and the lively Puerto del Carmen and Costa Teguise.

Population: 155,800
Nearest airports: Lanzarote Airport has a reasonable choice of flights to European cities during most of the year.
Pros: stunning landscape, beautiful beaches.
Cons: very busy in high season, hot and windy in the summer.
Property prices: less developed than Gran Canaria and Tenerife, Lanzarote also has cheaper prices, especially in the more popular resorts. Houses in Playa Blanca are considerably more expensive. New construction is limited.
Average square metre price (November 2021): €1,338

Canary Islands - Tenerife

The largest and most populated of the seven, Tenerife is the Canaries' most famous holiday destination and the most popular island with foreign property buyers. Like Gran Canaria, it has two contrasting halves: the south is arid, generally flat and with sandy beaches while the north is verdant and mountainous with a rugged coastline. Spain's highest mountain, El Teide (3,718m and snow-capped in winter), divides the two.

The south is home to resorts such as Los Cristianos and Playa de las Américas, popular package holiday destinations and more up-market resorts such as Costa Adeje. Santa Cruz de Tenerife, an interesting colonial city, has good amenities. La Laguna, a historic university town, is to the north where you'll also find the picturesque town of Puerto de la Cruz and the stunning Orotava Valley.

Population: 928,600
Nearest airports: Tenerife has two airports (North and South) and between them, they provide an excellent choice of direct flights to Europe and mainland Spain.
Pros: year-round pleasant climate, scenic surroundings especially in the north, good amenities.
Cons: very busy in high season, heavily developed in the south.
Property prices: vary considerably depending on the location. They're at their cheapest in resorts like Playa de las Américas and the most expensive in Costa Adeje and Puerto de la Cruz.
Average square metre price (November 2021): €2,682

Canary Islands - El Hierro, La Gomera and La Palma

The remotest and smallest islands have traditionally attracted few foreign property buyers. All are volcanic (La Palma suffered a particularly violent eruption in 2021) but while El Hierro is almost barren and windswept, La Palma and La Gomera have lush, green landscapes. Apart from the islands' capitals, there are few resorts on the islands.

Population: El Hierro – 11,100; La Gomera – 21,600; La Palma – 83,500
Nearest airports: all three have airports, but with domestic flights only.
Pros: quiet even in high season, warm weather year-round.
Cons: few international connections, could be too small for some people.
Property prices: limited construction and short supply ensure that properties keep their value although prices are lower than those on the other islands. Most properties are small detached homes with apartments available in the capitals and larger towns.

Connections

Connections include travel – how you get to and from Spain (and move around when you're there) – and online connectivity. The good news is that both are excellent in the most popular parts of Spain with foreign property buyers.

Travel connections

By air: Malaga and Alicante Airports are the fourth and sixth busiest in Spain with a wide range of direct flights to many European cities. You can also fly to Dubai and the US in high season from Malaga. Mallorca Airport has the third highest number of passengers in Spain, although flights are less frequent in the winter. And the airports on Tenerife and Gran Canaria both offer good connections with mainline Spain and Europe.

By train: Several of Spain's largest cities have high-speed AVE rail connections – for example, the AVE service between Malaga and Madrid, and Alicante and Madrid takes just 2.5 hours. Many areas have local train services (known as Cercanías) that provide an easy and inexpensive way of moving around. However, there are no train services on the islands. You can find out more about train services in Spain via the Renfe website (renfe.com/es/en).

By bus: Services vary from excellent in the most-populated areas to poor in more remote regions. Cities and large towns tend to have good and inexpensive local bus services (e.g. a flat rate of €1 for a single journey).

By road: Spain has a vast network of highways that connect most towns and cities, many of which are dual carriageway. There are also several toll motorways, particularly along the Mediterranean coast (AP-7). Fees tend to be high, but these roads are generally quick and safe. On the other hand, secondary roads are less well-maintained and Spain's remotest parts have poor road connections – you may find the only access is via a narrow and winding mountain track.

Online connections

Internet and mobile phone data connections tend to be good throughout Spain except in remote areas. High-speed internet (often fibre optic) is available in cities and towns. For mobiles, 4G is widely available and many cities now offer 5G connections.

Amenities

These include shops, bars and restaurants, leisure options, sports facilities, hospitals, schools and banks. In short, all those things you need for everyday life!

As in most countries, amenities in Spain vary depending on the size and population of the area. The Costa del Sol generally has excellent facilities, although they tend to be better to the west of Malaga city. Those on the Costa Blanca are also good, particularly around Alicante. In other cities and large towns, you'll generally find everything you need within walking distance.

On the islands, services and amenities tend to be concentrated in the more populated areas. For example, Palma de Mallorca offers a wide range, as does Las Palmas on Gran Canaria. Smaller towns have their limitations and in villages you may find very few amenities.

TOP TIP

Decide which amenities you need nearby (within walking distance or a 10-15-minute drive) and which you don't mind travelling some distance to reach. Then, when you're researching an area, locate your essential amenities on a map.

Tourism

Over 12% of Spain's annual GDP comes from tourism, making it one of the country's biggest industries. In 2019 (the latest 'normal' year for tourism), Spain welcomed almost 84 million foreign tourists, mostly to the Mediterranean coasts and the islands.

Most of Spain's resorts are popular tourist spots and many are favourites with both foreigners and Spanish visitors. As a result, their populations swell during high season (Easter and the summer) when services and amenities are stretched to their maximum. On the other hand, some resorts become ghost towns in the winter when amenities may shut down altogether.

However, there are also year-round holiday locations. They include the Costa del Sol and the Canary Islands.

If it's important for you to find out how tourism affects your chosen location, ask the locals. But most of all, visit in the summer and winter to see for yourself.

Price of property

Along with location, this is a major consideration when buying a property. While it's true that some parts of Spain still have bargain properties on the market, in most areas you'll find that getting cheap property isn't as easy as it was a decade ago. However, as always, prices depend on demand and when this is low, you will generally get more for your euros.

For more information on property prices, read our dedicated chapter on page 72.

DID YOU KNOW?

Purchase taxes and costs range from 8 to 13% of the property's price, adding considerably to your budget. These high expenses also mean that buying is only financially viable if you can recuperate the purchase costs, typically after at least five years.

Cost of living

Although cost of living has risen considerably over the last ten years, Spain remains relatively cheap, particularly when compared to most Northern European countries. This is especially true of food and drink, eating out and general entertainment.

There are, however, exceptions and prices in certain parts of Spain (e.g. Madrid and Barcelona) sit on a par with the equivalent in other large European cities. According to research by the Bank of Spain, Madrid and Barcelona are the most expensive places in the country. Living costs in both cities are up to 31% higher than the cheapest areas in Spain.

The map on the following page shows the cheapest (generally inland except for the Murcia Coast) and most expensive areas (the largest cities and on the islands). The cost of living in an area shaded mid-grey (e.g. the western Costa del Sol or Palma de Mallorca) is around 7% higher than a light grey area such as the Costa del Azahar.

0.95-1.00
0.85-0.95
0.80-0.85
0.75-0.80

But even in the most expensive areas it's possible to save money. For example:

- By shopping where the locals go (e.g. at weekly food markets) and not buying imported food.

- By walking or using public transport instead of a private car.

- By making use of discounts or freebies - for example, some cinemas have membership cards with lower ticket prices and many museums have open doors at least once a week.

TOP TIP

When buying a home, do all the Maths – work out the monthly expenses for the property (e.g. utilities, council taxes and community fees). Once you know the approximate costs, work out whether you can afford it.

Local economy

If you're buying in Spain with the view to relocating there, it's worth doing some research into the local economy. This is particularly important if you're planning to work as an employee or self-employed.

As in all countries, the economy in different areas of Spain moves at different paces. For example, Madrid, Barcelona and the Basque Country tend to perform better than the rest of Spain while Malaga province (Costa del Sol) generally registers higher growth than the rest of Andalusia.

Unemployment, often a benchmark for measuring how a local economy is doing, is traditionally high in Spain. In quarter 3 2021, the national jobless rate stood at 14.57%, although this figure hides big variations. In Madrid, it stood at 11.84%, while in Andalusia, unemployment was 22.41%.

At the time of writing, the Spanish economy was on the long road to recovery after the arrival of the Covid-19 pandemic. GDP plummeted by 10.8% in 2020 but bounced back in 2021. By quarter 3, year-on-year growth was at 2.7%. The European Commission predicts Spain's GDP will be 6.2% in 2021 and 6.3% in 2022.

Language

Language is an integral part of choosing what sort of community you'd like to live in. While it isn't always essential to learn Spanish if you're buying a home, being able to speak at least the basics will make your everyday life easier and less frustrating.

Learning to speak Spanish will also help you fit in with the local community, appreciate Spanish culture and probably open doors to you that might otherwise stay closed.

It's true that in areas popular with foreign holidaymakers, most locals speak some English, but you can't count on it. You need basic knowledge to help you understand your bills, deal with tradespeople and communicate with the Spanish authorities, e.g. your local council.

Cultural fit

This might seem a strange thing to consider because everyone needs to adapt to a new culture and most people aren't familiar with the Spanish way of thinking and doing things. But when you're thinking about a location, consider the following:

Option A: Do you want to immerse yourself in a totally Spanish experience?

Option B: Would you prefer to live among fellow expats much as you do in your home country (but in the sunshine!)?

Option C: Or would you prefer a combination of the two?

All three are possible, but not always in the same part of Spain.

Option A: If you're looking to enjoy the 'real' Spain and surround yourself with Spaniards, your best bet is to choose an inland location or a large city. That said, the cosmopolitan nature of Spain in the 21st century means you're likely to come across at least some foreigners.

Advantages: you'll experience and discover the real Spain and the true Spanish way of life.
Disadvantages: you'll need to learn to speak Spanish fluently to fit in and settling into a completely different culture from day one might be more challenging.

Option B: If you prefer to mix mostly with other expat homeowners, the islands, Costa del Sol and Costa Blanca are your oysters. Towns such as Ciudad Quesada on the southern Costa Blanca and Manilva on the western Costa del Sol have more foreign residents than Spaniards.

Advantages: you'll feel 'at home' straightaway and have no trouble communicating.
Disadvantages: expat communities can be claustrophobic, transient and feel as if you're living in a bubble.

Option C: If you're looking for the best of both worlds, try a larger resort such as Denia on the Costa Blanca or Marbella on the Costa del Sol. Coastal cities such as Valencia, Alicante and Malaga also provide a good mix of foreign and local residents.

RENTING BEFORE BUYING

What's inside this chapter

- How to find your rental property
- Rental regulations
- Information on rent-to-buy contracts

You may well be very familiar with Spain and already have a clear idea about where you want to buy. Or perhaps you like the general idea of Spain but don't know where to buy. In either case, it makes real sense to thoroughly explore the pros and cons of any area you like before you take the plunge and put a deposit on a property. You may be lucky and find the right location first time. However, you could also be unlucky and end up spending money on a home in the wrong place.

One of the best ways to avoid buying in the wrong location is to rent before you buy. This gives you the chance to explore the area and see if it works for you, to experience it at different times of the year and to decide if you like the idea of owning a property in Spain. And all without the big financial commitment involved in buying a house.

In this chapter, we look at how to find a rental property, what's in a long-term rental contract and the rent-to-buy option.

Location	Monthly rent per m^2	% increase in year
Spain	€10.50	-7.1%
Balearic Islands	€11.80	-1.8%
Barcelona city	€15.00	-4.5%
Canary Islands	€10.20	+1.6%
Costa de Almeria	€6.80	+3.1%
Costa del Azahar	€6.40	+5.2%
Costa Blanca	€7.30	+0.5%
Costa Brava	€10.00	+1.7%
Costa Calida	€6.70	+1.9%
Costa de la Luz	€7.70	-0.1%
Costa del Sol	€9.80	+1.6%
Costa Dorada	€7.60	+0.8%
Costa Verde	€7.60	+3.1%
Madrid city	€14.80	-6.0%

(Source: Idealista, October 2021)

How to find a rental property

Online portals

Many property portals offer platforms for owners and estate agents to advertise their homes. There isn't really much difference between them, although you might a the same property is cheaper on one portal than on another.

Need to know about online portals

- Agents advertise on them as well as private owners, but it might not be obvious they are agents (and they will charge a fee).

- Photos may not be authentic or accurate so don't be surprised to find that the property is very different from the photos when you view it.

- All offer comprehensive filters so you can narrow down your search.

Six largest portals for rental properties

- Idealista (idealista.com/en/)- the largest and with an English-language version.
- Fotocasa (fotocasa.es/en/) - 2nd largest and with an English-language version.
- Habitaclia (habitaclia.com)- smaller selection, with holiday lets and in English.
- Pisos.com - smaller and with an English-language version.
- En Alquiler (enalquiler.com/en) - specialised in long-term rentals and in English.
- Mitula (mitula.com) - holiday let search option and in Spanish only.

Property finders

Also known as personal property shoppers, these people are experts in an area and work for you as opposed to an agent or owner. They usually charge a set fee rather than commission on a sale.

If you decide to use a property finder, make sure you have an exact list of what you're looking for in a rental property and understand the fees (and what they include) from the start.

To source a property finder, ask around for recommendations or search 'property finder in (your chosen location)'.

Estate agents

Not all estate agents handle rental properties so you may need to visit a few to find one that does. Expect to pay one month's rent or 10% of the annual rent as fees. Be aware that the amount may not include IVA (VAT) at 21%.

How to rent a property

Once you've chosen a property, you need to reserve it. This is usually done by paying a fee of one month's rent (deductible from later payments). You then sign the rental contract (see below) and pay the first month's rent, security deposit (1 to 2 months' rent) and, if applicable, the agency fee (1 month's rent or 10% of the annual rent plus 21% VAT).

Rental contracts

Spanish law generally favours tenants over landlords, but both parties have a series of obligations. The contract sets out the basics and you can agree other conditions in the contract as well. It should be in Spanish, so make sure you understand every clause (and its implications) before you sign on the dotted line.

Length of rental

Under the law passed in 2019, you are allowed to stay in the rental for a minimum of 5 years (7 if the owner of the property is a company). You don't have to leave the property before the 5 years unless – and this is the only reason – the landlord needs it for a close relative (spouse, child or parent) to live in. However, your landlord can only apply this rule after at least 1 year of your tenancy and must give you 2 months' notice. This option must be clearly stated in the contract.

Longer rentals

If after 5 years your landlord doesn't want you to remain in the property, they must give you 4 months' notice before the contract expires. Otherwise, the contact can be extended by annual periods for up to 3 further years.

Giving notice

You must stay for a minimum of 6 months in the property. After that, you must then give the landlord 30 days' notice before you wish to leave.

Paying rent

You must usually pay your rent between the 1st and 5th of each calendar month. Ask your landlord for a receipt for every monthly payment – a copy of the bank transfer may not be enough if you have legal problems.

Rent rises

During the 5 years' rental, the landlord may increase your rent every year by the official rate of inflation (Índice de Precios de Consumo/IPC in Spanish and published every month by the government). Both parties must agree to this and include this provision in the contract.

This rental increase only applies to the 5-year minimum rental period. After that, both parties must agree a new rental rate.

Deposits

Minimum 1 month's rent and maximum 2.

Payment of expenses

Properties are liable for taxes and fees including community charges (if your long-term rental is an apartment or part of the complex) and local council taxes. These are usually paid by the landlord, but both parties can agree that the tenant pays them. In towns that charge a separate refuse collection tax (e.g. Fuengirola), the tenant usually pays this.

Tenants pay utility charges (water, electricity, gas, telephone, internet connection, etc). Make sure the contract states exactly who is responsible for paying what.

Maintenance of the property

Under Spanish law, the landlord must carry out all maintenance to keep the property habitable except when the tenant causes damage. In practice, this means that the landlord is responsible for maintaining and repairing pipes, walls, ceilings and floors, and the tenant is responsible for repairs of blinds, locks, taps, toilets and paintwork.

Improvements to the property

If the landlord invests in improvements, he/she can charge the tenant for these in monthly installments. However, the charge cannot be more than 20% of the regular monthly rent and only applies after a minimum stay period of 5 years.

Again, this is open to negotiation and the law states that both parties can freely agree that the improvements made during the first 5 years can be charged to the tenant and without the limit of 20% of the rent. But this must be a clear agreement and incorporated into the contract.

However, other improvements made during the first 5 years are open to negotiation. The law states that both parties can agree on what improvements can be charged to the tenant without a limit of 20% of the rent. Again, there must be a clear agreement in the contract.

Work on the property

To make any improvements to the property, however small, you need written permission from your landlord. Otherwise, the landlord may cancel the contract and you could be obliged to restore everything to its original state.

Sub-letting the property

Unless your contract says otherwise, you cannot sub-let the property.

Alternative use for the property

Unless your contract states otherwise, the property cannot be used for anything other than living in so, for example, you can't open a business in it. (Working from home is obviously an exception.)

Inventories

Most long-term rentals come partially or fully furnished. Make sure the landlord prepares an inventory of all contents in the property, check it carefully and then attach it to the contract. Both parties should sign the inventory.

Checking damage

You usually have 30 days after you move in to check for damage, things that don't work etc and report it to the landlord.

Utilities

Electricity and water supplies are usually registered and connected in rental properties. Some have gas (mainline in modern properties, gas bottles in older properties) for heating water.

Read the meters

On your first day of rental, check the electricity, water and gas meters and take note of the readings. You can then negotiate with your landlord when the first bill arrives to avoid paying for the previous tenant's consumption.

Paying utility bills

You have 2 options:

1. **In your name:** Payment of utilities in your name and via direct debit through your bank account. To do this for gas and electricity you need to contact the utility company and provide your NIE (Número de Identificación de Extranjero – see page 104), new bank details and the number of the utility contract. You can contact the companies by phone or online – many have virtual offices. Note that most agents at utility companies don't usually speak English and websites tend to be in Spanish only.
2. **In your landlord's name:** Your landlord pays the bills and charges you for them separately – ask to see the bills and keep a copy for your records. Some landlords prefer this option.

Rent to buy

It is possible that the property you choose to rent turns out to be perfect for you and as a result, you want to buy it. There is a rental contract option that allows you to rent a property and then have the option to buy it if you decide at a later date that it's the property for you. This type of contract is known as *contrato de arrendamiento con opción de compra*.

How does it work?

A rent-to-buy contract contains the usual rental rights and obligations (e.g. rental rate, length of the contract, conditions to cancel etc). It also has a specific clause that includes the option for the tenants to buy the property. This clause states:

- The price of the property.
- The timeframe you have as a tenant to exercise your right to purchase.

The price can be fixed or left open and described, for example, as "market price at the time the purchase option is exercised".

The rent-to-buy contract may include a premium clause, which is an extra price you pay for having the right to purchase. If you buy, the premium is discounted from the final price of the property. If you don't, the owner keeps the premium. Like most clauses in rental contracts, the premium clause isn't obligatory.

Do I pay more rent if I have a rent-to-buy contract?

Not necessarily and only if a premium is agreed and stated in the premium clause (see above).

Are rental fees included in the price?

Yes, usually your monthly rental payments are discounted from the final price you pay. So, if the agreed purchase price is €150,000 and you have paid €8,000 in rent when you decide to buy, you will pay €142,000 for the property.

What if I decide not to buy or can't buy when the deadline arrives, can the contract be extended?

Yes, if both parties agree. Your landlord might decide to renew your rental contract but without the right to purchase option.

Who pays expenses in a rental contract with the option to buy?

As in all rental contracts, it depends on what is mutually agreed. Usually, the landlord pays for local council taxes and community fees and the tenant pays for utilities and refuse collection tax (if applicable).

WHAT SORT OF PROPERTY TO BUY?

What's inside this chapter

- A guide to the types of property
- Pros and cons of buying an apartment, townhouse, villa, country house or plot

Once you've worked out your budget and identified your preferred location, it's time to decide what sort of property to buy (new-build or resale). In this section, you'll find a brief description of the main types of homes on the market in Spain. Plus, we've listed the pros and cons of each one.

New-build properties

Most areas popular with foreign buyers have a selection of new properties on the market. The exceptions are the main islands in the Balearics and Canaries where new construction has all but come to a halt.

Elsewhere, you'll find a good choice of new properties. New builds tend to be more expensive - for example, on the Costa del Sol in quarter 2 2021, they cost over 30% more per square metre than resale properties. In addition, prices have risen sharply over the last few years, particularly since the arrival of the pandemic and, with it, increased demand for larger, more modern homes.

Pros

- No refurbishment or renovation is required.
- You can often choose fixtures and fittings.
- And the property is move-in or rental ready.

Cons

- If you buy off plan, you'll have to wait for completion (often as long as 24 months).
- Possible problems with delays in completion or the finished property not being what you were originally sold.

DID YOU KNOW?

Buying a home from a developer involves a different purchase process – see Purchase Procedure on page 102 for information – and there are additional guarantees and checks your lawyer should make before you commit to buying.

Apartments & flats

These are by far the most common type of property in Spain (most Spaniards live in an *apartamento* or *piso*) and you'll find apartment blocks everywhere except in small villages. In some resort areas such as Benidorm and Fuengirola, apartments make up almost all of the property market!

The quality of construction and finishes varies hugely. At one end, you'll find blocks built in the 1960s with cramped accommodation and antiquated plumbing and electrical systems and at the other, recently-finished complexes that house smart homes built with sustainable materials. In general, the cheaper the apartment, the more you'll need to do to refurbish it.

All apartments share communal facilities and services, whose upkeep owners pay for via community fees. See page 69 for more information.

TOP TIP

Always ask about monthly community fees before you buy. Make sure you know exactly what they include and decide whether they're worth it for you. If you aren't going to make full use of the pool, for example, it makes financial sense to pay lower fees in a property without one.

Pros

- Apartments are generally the cheapest properties on the market.
- They're easy to maintain.
- They're convenient for holiday homes because you can lock-up and go.
- They're secure, especially if they have 24-hour security.
- And many have communal facilities such as gardens that you can enjoy without having to look after them.

Cons

- Apartments can be expensive to own if community fees are high.
- The community may be poorly maintained or conflictive.
- Communal facilities may be inadequate for the number of residents, especially during the summer.
- And sound insulation is usually poor, meaning you'll probably hear your neighbours next-door, upstairs and downstairs!

FACTS ABOUT PROPERTY IN SPAIN

Estimated number of properties in Spain - 25.8 million
Region with the highest number - Andalusia with 4.46 million
Estimated number of new builds in Spain - 456,918 (1.77% of total)
Provinces with the most new builds:
Barcelona - 43,000
Alicante (Costa Blanca) - 36,864

(Source: Ministry of Transport, Mobility and Urban Agenda 2020)

Average age of property in Spain - 45 years old
Most property was built in the 1980s
Barcelona province has the oldest property on average (1960)
Toledo province has the youngest on average (2003)

(Source: Idealista property portal, 2021)

Townhouses

Rows of terraced houses (*casa adosada*), often with three or four floors, are commonplace in many parts of Spain, particularly in resort areas and in the suburbs of large cities. They tend to be spacious and often include a basement for use as a garage and storage. They sometimes come with a small private garden and many have rooftop terraces.

Quality varies, but as this type of property is relatively recent (few were built before the 90s), it's unlikely to need major refurbishment. Most townhouses form part of a larger complex and share communal facilities such as a pool and garden. Some developments are gated with security services.

Pros

- Townhouses give you plenty of space for both you and your belongings.
- They're more private than apartments.
- You can use communal facilities without having to look after them yourself.
- And this type of property is generally low maintenance.

Cons

- Your neighbours (on both sides) could be noisy or difficult.
- Communities aren't always well-maintained.
- And multi-floor living isn't ideal if you have mobility problems (or don't like stairs!).

Villas

Villas (*chalet* or *villa*) are part and parcel of resorts in Spain, and mostly built to meet demand from Spanish and foreign holidaymakers. That means you won't find many outside coastal and resort areas. In contrast, villas dominate some parts of the coast such as Moraira on the Costa Blanca or Ibiza.

The age, size and quality of villas varies hugely. You can buy a small home built in the late 60s needing full refurbishment or a modern mansion that's move-in-ready. Some properties form part of complexes sharing communal facilities such as gardens and a pool, while others sit on independent plots.

Pros

- You get maximum privacy.
- You can often tailor the home to your specific needs.
- And if the plot is big enough, you can extend your living space.

Cons

- Maintenance is high and can be expensive.
- Security can be an issue unless the villa is inside a gated community.
- And running costs are much higher than an apartment or townhouse.

Country homes

If you're looking for a home away from the coasts and resorts, a country home (*finca*) could be for you. They range from a shepherd's cottage to a large farmhouse with just about anything in between. Some are built in local traditional style such as a the *cortijos* in Andalusia, *masías* in Catalonia and the Balearic Islands or *pazos* in Galicia.

Most country homes are older properties (at least 50 years old – some date back several centuries) and will almost always need considerable refurbishment. The majority come with land that may be arable (e.g. olive or citrus groves) or pasture.

Rural properties often come with legal issues and are potentially the most problematic type of Spanish property, so take independent legal advice before committing to a purchase. And make sure your lawyer is aware of any intended refurbishment plans to ensure they are possible because in many parts of rural Spain, you can't automatically renovate a ruin, for example.

Pros

- You get a lot of property and land for your money.
- You can enjoy peace and quiet with no noisy neighbours.
- And you can live in some of Spain's most beautiful scenery.

Cons

- Refurbishment may not be possible and if it is, it will be expensive.
- Maintenance costs are high.
- And amenities may be some distance away, making a car is essential.

Plots

You may perhaps want to start from scratch and build your own home to your specifications and requirements. The good news is that plots of land are available in most resort areas where you'll also find a reputable network of architects and builders. But as in all countries, building a property in Spain is probably one of the most stressful ways to buy a home.

Plots vary in size and this, in turn, determines how big the build can be. They also vary hugely in price, with premium land in resort areas costing over €1,000 per square metre. Some come landscaped and build-ready, while others don't even have utility connections.

Pros

- You have a blank space to build on and create your dream home.
- Land is generally a good investment and appreciates over time.
- And you can build a home more cheaply than buying the same finished equivalent.

Cons

- Planning regulations may limit how much you can build.
- Prime land is expensive.
- And you need to be patient while the design, construction and paperwork processes go ahead.

DID YOU KNOW?

Planning permission isn't automatically granted for a plot and depending on the land's classification, you might not be able to build at all. Use independent legal services to check for you.

10 things to consider (very carefully) before you buy a plot

The information in this section was generously provided by Alejandro Jiménez, architect at CMYK Arquitectos (cmyk-arq.es).

See How to choose a good architect on page 86 and Building your own home on page 63 for more information.

Before you sign on the dotted line for a piece of land you've fallen in love with, get professional advice from an independent lawyer and architect for the following:

- Check the plot's classification – to be able to build on it, it must be within "buildable urban limits" (*suelo urbano consolidado*/SUC in Spanish). If it isn't, you won't get building permission.

- Check the plot's infrastructure, e.g. road and pavement access and utility connections. If they don't exist, you'll have to pay for them.

- Make sure the land doesn't come under any local planning regulations such as coastal protection areas and protected natural spaces Check too that there's no designated public use (e.g. for roads or railways). If there is, you're unlikely to get a building permit and it will be difficult to register the finished property in your name.

- Take a good look at local planning regulations to determine what you can build on the plot, e.g. permitted build size and height, and how much space you must leave for the boundaries.

- Look at the plot's gradient and bear in mind that building on steep plots is more difficult and expensive than on flat ones. On the other hand, an incline means you can enjoy the views without other properties getting in the way.

- Check the plot's orientation and avoid north-facing plots on slopes (you'll never get any sun). The best plots have potential for south or south-east/west facing living spaces.

- Get a rough idea of the characteristics of the ground to find out how difficult it will be to lay foundations or if you'll be able to build a basement.

- Get an idea of the project's total cost to find out if you can afford the plot. Your architect can give you an estimate so you can do your Maths. Note that banks rarely approve mortgage loans for building plots.

- Find out if the seller is an individual or a company. Generally speaking, taxes are lower if you buy from an individual. For example, in Andalusia if the seller is a company you'll pay 21% tax (as VAT) whereas if the vendor is an individual, you'll pay 7% transfer tax. The 14% difference could mean a saving or additional expense of thousands of euros.

- Find out if the plot has any charges or debts on it. Check public rights of way on the land e.g. an underground utility supply (gas or water pipe, for example). This isn't usually a major problem, but it's good to know because you must give the company access for repair if there's a fault.

BUILDING A PROPERTY IN SPAIN

What's inside this chapter

- How to find the right architect
- Information on the construction process & timeline
- What it costs to build a property

Rather than buying an off-plan or resale property, you might prefer to build a home from scratch. Maybe there's nothing on the market to suit your requirements or perhaps you've fallen in love with a plot. Of course, a self-build allows you to own a home that fits your specifications exactly and it can be cheaper than the equivalent property already on the market.

But as you'll know from watching programmes like *Grand Design* on television, building your own home is rarely straightforward, keeping to the original budget can be a challenge and it usually takes longer than planned.

We've already looked at things to bear in mind when buying a plot — see page 61 for a reminder of those — so this chapter dives into the nitty-gritty of a build. It looks at how to find a good architect, the steps and timeline involved in the process and how much it all costs.

Much of the information in this chapter has been generously provided by Alejandro Jiménez from CMYK Arquitectos.

How to find the right architect

Spain is renowned for its fine architectural designers and many highly-regarded foreign architects also work in the country, so finding a good one for your project won't be a problem. But you don't want just a competent architect, you want the right one for you. You need a professional who understands your requirements, your concerns and your lifestyle. Matching these with a house design is usually a case of personal connection and architects often become friends with their clients as a result.

TOP TIP

Houzz.com is a good place to start looking for an architect. Go to the Find Professionals tab, select Architects and Building Designers and then add your chosen location.

Initial search

Recommendations are always a good place to start. But be aware that a recommended architect might not fit in with your style even though your friend couldn't be happier with their new home. Online searches can also be helpful and when you come across a possible candidate note the following:

- **Website** — is it well-structured and easy to understand? If it is, the chances are that the architect is a good communicator.

- **Language** – do they speak yours or one you understand well? Communication, an essential part of designing a home, will be difficult if they don't.

- **Professional track record** – look at how long the architect has been in business, where and what they have designed. Do they specialise in the type of project you're looking for or do they design a range of products?

- **Portfolio** – spend some time looking at this to find out if you like the architect's designs.

- **Reviews** – check they're genuine first (if possible, get client contact details) and then read them.

Short list

Once you have a list of several possible candidates, it's time to narrow the search down:

First, arrange a meeting with the architect. Explain your ideas carefully and what you're looking for and need in the home. Does the architect listen and take what you're saying on board? Or do they try to impose their own ideas and criteria?

Second, analyse how you felt at the meeting. Did you like the architect and did you feel you could work with them? If the answer to either of those questions is no, cross this architect off your list – you'll be working together for 19 to 24 months, so there needs to be a good personal connection.

Third, get an estimate of fees from each one candidate. When comparing, make sure you know exactly what each estimate includes. Is it:

- Just the design?
- The design and extra services such as getting licences and help finding a builder and technical architect?
- The whole package including topographical survey, structural calculations and cost of licences?

TOP TIP

Architectural fees are not fixed in Spain, so be prepared for a range of estimates. In general terms, allow for 10-12% of the cost of building the home. Remember that this figure excludes the builder's fees, taxes and associated costs. Don't be tempted to go for a ridiculously low estimate because it probably reflects a lower standard of services and professionalism, which in home design can lead to serious issues.

The construction process and timeline

Building a home is rarely a quick process anywhere. In Spain, it usually takes between 18 and 24 months as follows:

1. **Finding the plot** – a vital first step and one that can take 3 to 6 months including viability studies.
2. **Getting a loan** – around 90% of Spaniards building their own homes get mortgage financing, but among foreigners, the percentage is much lower. Bear in mind that not all banks offer this type of loan and that getting approval takes time. The preparatory study alone takes at least a month.
3. **Finding a reliable architect** – obviously essential to build the home you want and avoid unpleasant surprises. It can take up to 3 months to find one you like and trust.
4. **Designing the project** – usually divided into two parts: concept design and final design. You'll have a lot of input into the concept, which usually takes 2 to 3 months to come together. The final design has a similar timeline.
5. **Getting the building permit** – generally applied for in tandem with the concept design and the timeline depends on the local council. In small towns, expect it to take 3 months while in larger areas, e.g. Malaga, it's more likely to be 6 months or longer (in Marbella, for example, allow at least up to a year).
6. **Choosing the builder** – once the final design is ready, it's time to get estimates for the building work. As with architect fees, a low estimate isn't always the best option. Bear in mind the builder's track record and previous work (if possible, make a visit) and ask for references. Allow 1 to 2 months for this, which you can go ahead with while the permits are being approved.
7. **Building your home** – there are various parts to this as follows:
- Preparing the plot, moving earth etc – 1 month.
- Foundations – 1-2 months depending on the ground.
- Structure – 4-6 months for traditional reinforced concrete with pillars; 2 months for industrial steel structure.
- Outside and inside walls – 2-3 months.
- Finishes – 2-3 months.

No of months	1	2	3	4	5	6	7	8	9	10	11	12	13	14	15	16	17	18	19	20	21	22	23	24
PLOT	■	■	■																					
LOAN		■	■																					
ARCHITECT			■	■																				
PROJECT					■	■	■	■																
LICENCES								■	■	■														
BUILDER									■	■														
CONSTRUCTION											■	■	■	■	■	■	■	■	■	■	■	■	■	
DOCUMENTATION																								■

The costs of building your own home

This section gives you a rough idea of how much you can expect to pay. To do this, we've taken as our base a **200-400m² detached home** (including basement) and with no build complexity. Note that we haven't included the builder's fees.

Architect's fees

As we mentioned earlier, fees are not regulated and you may find a wide range when you ask for estimates. Big-name architects will obviously charge more and there'll be some small practices whose fees are very low (which may reflect the quality of their work and services).

As an idea, expect an estimate of **€20,000-30,000** (plus 21% VAT).

Technical architect's fees

Under Spanish law, you must employ a technical architect (*arquitecto técnico*) to supervise the technical and structural aspects of the build.

Their fees are usually 30% of the architect's, so allow for **€6,000 to €9,000** (plus 21% VAT).

Construction costs

These vary depending on the materials you've chosen for your home.

In our example detached home, they'll be in the range of **€180,000 to €240,000**.

Fees and taxes

- **Planning fees** (tasa urbanística) – they depend on the council and are a percentage of the build price or a coefficient of the property's size. Allow for **€1,500 to €2,500**.

- **Building tax** (impuesto de construcciones, instalaciones y obras(ICIO) – it varies from region to region but is usually 3-4% of the build cost. Budget for **€4,500 to €6,000**.

Additional costs

- Topographical survey - **€400-500** (plus 21% VAT)

- Geotechnical survey - **€700-900** (plus 21% VAT)

- Architect's licence for the project and completion certificate - **€300-400** (plus 21% VAT)

- Structural calculations - **€400-600** (plus 21% VAT)

- Building standards compliance - **€300-400** (plus 21% VAT)

Total estimated costs* for a 200-400m² detached home

€214,100 to €290,300 (*not including the cost of the plot, builder's fees or VAT).

COMMUNITIES OF OWNERS

What's inside this chapter

- What a community of owners is
- What it involves
- Typical costs of fees

If the property you buy in Spain shares common elements with any other property, it forms part of a community of property owners (*comunidad de propietarios*). This concept is similar to condominium properties in the US or tenement properties in some parts of the UK.

These shared elements might be limited to an entrance hall, lift and corridors or include gardens, pools, a gym, tennis courts and a co-working space.

In practice, most Spanish properties (all apartments, most townhouses and even many villas) form part of a community of property owners. The only properties that don't are detached houses on individual plots in public streets or homes on rural land.

This section answers frequently asked questions about communities of owners in Spain.

TOP TIP

Ask to see a copy of the last community of owners Annual General Meeting. This will give you the heads-up on any problems and an overview of whether things are friendly or acrimonious among the neighbours!

If I buy a property on a community of owners, what does this involve for me?

As an owner in a community of property owners, you own the property plus a share of the common elements. How much you pay for your share is calculated from the size of your property.

In addition to paying your quota of fees, you must follow and abide by all the community regulations (see below).

What are community fees?

The amount you pay contributes towards the upkeep and improvement of the common elements. How much you pay depends on the size of your property (the larger the property, the more you pay) and the extent of the facilities (the more there are, the higher the fees).

Fees are paid in instalments, e.g. monthly, quarterly or every six months.

Costs might be low, for example, €30 a month for an apartment with lift maintenance and cleaning of the entrance hall and corridors. Or they could be as high as €1,500 a month for a penthouse on a complex with a concierge, security and extensive facilities such as gardens and a pool.

Who decides how much owners pay?

The exact amount is calculated based on the community's annual expenses and determined at the annual general meeting of the community of owners.

Can the fees change?

Yes, if a majority of owners decides to modify fees at the annual general meeting. Extra fees can also be charged for improvements such as installing a larger lift, essential maintenance like painting the façade, or legal requirements, e.g. putting up a safety fence around a pool.

What about community rules?

Most communities of owners have rules and these are set out in the community's statutes. They include things like:

- Timetables for using facilities such as the pool and tennis courts.
- Noise regulations.
- Whether the community allows pets,
- If it permits holiday lets (some communities don't allow owners to let their properties).
- The colour approved for awnings.
- If you can cover your terrace or balcony.
- And if you can put laundry out to dry on your balcony.

How can I find out about the community fees and rules?

Before you buy, ask to see a copy of the community of owners statutes to check for any regulations that may affect you (e.g. prohibition of holiday lets). Your lawyer will find out about community fees.

PROPERTY PRICES IN SPAIN

What's inside this chapter

- Property market history
- Where to find information on prices
  Predictions for the future

Along with location, price counts as the other important factor when buying property, making this an essential chapter! In it, we take a look at the last 20 years in the Spanish property market and examine some of the underlying trends. We then provide some valuable resources for information on prices, both asking (the price the owner advertises) and actual (the price the buyer paid).

And finally, we get out the crystal ball and offer some hints on where the market might be going next. But this section has a small caveat: don't expect any firm predictions – we can only suggest general trends because, as the pandemic has taught us, there's no predicting anything for sure nowadays!

The last 20 years

As with many property markets worldwide, the Spanish market has had a rollercoaster ride since 2000. In just over two decades, prices have climbed to their highest in mid-2007 before sinking downwards and then slowly making their way up again. However, despite their recovery, they're still currently more than 30% below their 2007 peak.

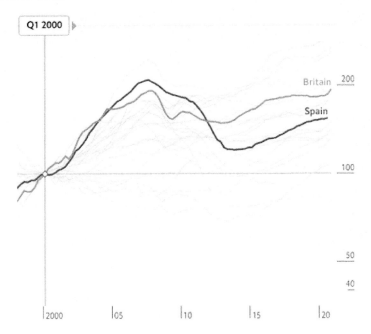

(Source: national statistics, OECD, The Economist)

The skyrocket

The new millennium started with a return to rising prices after a recession in the mid-90s. Prices quickly gained ground and yearly increases of over 20% were common in some parts of the country such as the Costa del Sol. New construction surged as over 800,000 new units were built a year between 2004 and 2006 and sales reached their height in 2007, when almost 800,000 homes changed hands.

The plummet

In 2008 the Lehmann Brothers and subprime crises arrived and the Spanish property market bubble burst with a loud pop. Foreign investment all but left the country, sales plummeted (in 2013, only 312,500 transactions took place) and prices went into a downward spiral. 2014 saw the market hit rock-bottom with prices 73% below the peak they had registered just 7 years earlier.

The second coming

Since then, prices have begun the long climb upwards, although progress hasn't been uniform and Spain still has markets moving at different speeds. In general terms, recovery has been quicker in the largest cities and areas popular with foreign buyers such as the islands (Balearic and Canary), Costa Blanca and Costa del Sol.

However, in others such as small provincial cities and coastlines with excess supply, e.g. the Costa del Azahar, Costa Brava and Murcia, prices still lag far behind their 2007 peak.

Property price highs and lows 2007 to 2021

Area	Highest price per m^2*	Lowest price per m^2**	Price per m^2 in Q2 2021	Difference highest and Q2 2021
Spain	€2,048	€1,197	€1,421	-30.6%
Balearic Islands	€2,729	€1,086	€2,442	-10.5%
Barcelona	€4,441	€2,205	€3,359	-24.4%
Canary Islands	€1,910	€1,060	€1,399	-26.2%
Costa Blanca	€1,977	€1,074	€1,204	-39.1%
Costa Brava	€2,672	€1,260	€1,492	-44.2%
Costa Calida	€1,743	€643	€1,001	-42.6%
Costa de Almeria	€1,915	€917	€940	-50.9%
Costa de la Luz	€2,076	€1,214	€1,330	-36.0%
Costa del Azahar	€1,790	€616	€995	-46.7%
Costa del Sol	€2,537	€1,274	€1,703	-32.9%
Madrid	€3,974	€1,621	€3,088	-22.3%

*2007-8
**2014-1015
(Q2 = April to June)
(Source: Tinsa, based on market valuations)

As the table above clearly shows, property prices in Spain are on average still around a third below their 2007-2008 peak. Even in areas where recovery has been more robust, e.g. Madrid and Barcelona, property remains up to a quarter cheaper. Only in the Balearic Islands are prices approaching their 2007-2008 maximum.

Note, however, that the above figures provide a general picture only and don't show localised statistics. So, for example, in Malaga city prices were 25.2% below their peak in the second quarter of 2021 compared to 32.9% for the Costa del Sol generally.

However, they do give you a good idea of trends over the last 15 years. Plus, you can see that in some parts of Spain – for example, Murcia – prices were almost two-thirds cheaper in 2014 than they were 7 years earlier.

DID YOU KNOW?

The Costa del Sol has the most properties on the market for at least €1 million in Spain (23.1% of the total), followed by the Balearic Islands with 22.9%. When it comes to price tags over €3 million, the Costa del Sol has 36.8% of the country's total and the Balearic Islands, 32.2%. (Figures based on asking prices on the Idealista portal in August 2021)

Location, location, location

Apart from the size and quality of a property, location has the most influence on its price. The closer a property is to a city or resort, the more expensive it is. You can expect to pay three to four times more for an apartment in Marbella or Palma de Mallorca than you would in on the Costa del Azahar or the Mar Menor, for example.

Homes with a beachfront position or overlooking a golf course also attract a premium. However, properties in a good location keep their value better than those in a less desirable situation.

Where to get information

Unlike some countries such as the US where property statistics are easy to come by and highly detailed, Spanish data is less comprehensive. There are, however, some good sources of information and by comparing several of them, you can get a picture of market trends.

Official statistics

These are available from several different sources including:

- **Ministry of Transport, Mobility and Urban Agenda** (mitma.gob.es) – data is available (in Spanish only) for property based on valuations and land based on actual prices. You can consult data for regions, provinces and municipalities with over 25,000 inhabitants, downloadable in Excel spreadsheet form.

- **Notaries Association** (notariado.org)– data for sales and prices (in Spanish only) is published periodically and generally only for regional or provincial level. Information is based on actual prices paid when signing the title deeds at a notary.

- **Registrars Association** (registradores.org) – figures are based on data from property transactions and provide quarterly data (in Spanish only) on several property transactions including prices, sales and nationality of buyers in regions and provinces.

Property portals

Idealista (idealista.com/en)– publishes price statistics. Choose your region, province, municipality and district and click on 'Consult report'. You then get prices for the current month, the previous month and 12 months ago. These statistics are based on asking prices, i.e. what the seller wanted for the property when they advertised it on the portal.

Valuation portals

Tinsa, Spain's largest valuations company (tinsa.es) – publishes monthly property price statistics (in Spanish only). It covers regions, provinces and provincial capitals. Select the location and a timeline appears showing price trends for the last 20 years. These statistics are based on market valuations, i.e. the price deemed the current market value by a professional valuer.

Future prices

And now to future price trends in Spain. As we said at the beginning and as we all know, upcoming trends are notoriously difficult to predict. However, there are usually reliable signs of a future bubble or crash – whether buyers take any notice of them or not is another matter!. For example, in 2005, the Bank of Spain and *The Economist* both warned of overheating in the market and 3 years later, it started to nosedive.

The underlying trend is always up

It's first worth pointing out that although property markets go up and down, the price trends always move upwards. The graph below clearly shows this underlying trend in both the Spanish and UK markets since 1975. So yes, both markets have seen booms and busts, but both have been going up for the last 50-odd years.

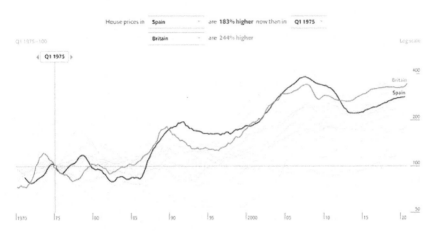

(Source: national statistics, OECD, The Economist)

Still a big gap to close

Data for the Spanish property market over the last two decades clearly shows the highs and lows, and how prices in most areas still have plenty of room to grow before they reach their 2007 peak.

And recent increases show that prices are generally growing slowly. According to Tinsa, they went up on average by 5.2% in the year to August 2021 (based on valuations). However, the rise was higher on the islands (7.9%) and lower in the largest cities (3.8%).

Strong demand at national and international level

One of the factors behind rising prices is demand. In common with many countries, Spain has seen a sharp rise in demand for homes since summer 2020. This is partly because of the desire among Spanish families for bigger homes as a result of the pandemic. There's also pent-up demand from foreign buyers who were unable to travel to Spain to buy property between March 2020 and summer 2021.

Sales went up by 26.2% nationally in the year to September 2021. The increase was even higher in some regions – for example, Andalusia (28.2%) and Galicia (30%)..
The uptick in sales in the second quarter was the highest quarterly rise since Q2

2008 and new-build properties are experiencing particularly high increases – for instance, on the Costa del Sol, sales went up by 23.6% in the year to September 2021 with those for new builds rising by 48.3%.

The Property Activity Index (Índice de Actividad Registral Inmobiliaria/ IARI), published by the Registrars Association), confirmed high levels of activity in Q2 2021. The Index rose by over 20% to reach 117.8, its highest level since the beginning of 2008.

Low interest rates

Mortgage loans are another consideration when forecasting future price trends. The Euribor (the European Central Bank benchmark rate for mortgages) has been below zero since March 2016. In September 2021, it stood at 0% and there are signs of upward movement. However, the rise is likely to be slow and gradual.

Low interest rates make for cheap mortgages, a major incentive behind many property purchases in Spain. As a result, loans went up by 48.9% in the year to July 2021 and mortgages formed part of 53.9% of all sales. In some parts of Spain, there was an even higher rise – in Catalonia, they went up by 82.3%, in the Comunidad Valenciana by 62.3% and on the Balearic Islands by 51.6%.

With no real sign that the Euribor will rise sharply, it follows that cheap mortgages will continue to drive demand and lead to an increase in prices.

The right time to buy?

And lastly, the million-euro question. Given current demand, low interest rates and the gap between peak and current prices, 2021-22 would appear to be a good time to buy. However, it's important to note that buying in Spain is a long-term project (at least 10 years) because:

- Buying costs are high (8-13% of the purchase price).
- Unless you're lucky (and can take the big financial risk), it's difficult to speculate on properties in Spain nowadays and make a profit.
- The gap between the highest and current prices is still wide in most parts of Spain. For example, if you bought on the Costa de la Luz in 2007 and wanted to sell now, you could get 36% less for your property. (See the table on page 74.)

TOP TIP

Deciding when to buy depends on your finances and market trends. But if you find the right property in the right place that offers you what you want, the right time to buy is now!

PROFESSIONALS TO HELP YOU BUY

What's inside this chapter

How to find the right person to help with each stage of the buying process

Only a buyer who's fluent in Spanish, familiar with Spanish property law and building structure, and an expert in Spanish paperwork could buy a home without the help of any professionals. They would also have to be extremely lucky, and even then, they wouldn't be able to purchase without a notary.

Bottom line? As well as this ebook, you're going to need people to help you.

In this chapter, we look at who these professionals are and explain what they do. For information on how much these professionals charge, see page 79.

How to find a professional

When looking for a good professional in a particular field, ask for recommendations from people you trust. Once you have a shortlist, Google each one to see if any red flags come up, get in touch and gauge the response you get.

A competent expert will come highly recommended, have a clean record on the internet and respond to your query promptly. Check also that your chosen professional is a member of the appropriate association.

Lawyer (*abogado*)

We've placed legal experts at the top of the list because we think using the services of an independent lawyer is an absolute must. This is because we've heard of so many buyers who have had problems with their purchase because they didn't have the right legal advice.

And when we say 'right' legal advice, we mean trained, registered, experienced and independent:

Trained – should have a Spanish degree in law (or a recognised foreign equivalent) and specialise in Spanish property law.

Registered – must be a member of a lawyers association (known as Colegio de Abogados) in the province where they are based, for example, Malaga for the Costa del Sol. Membership is compulsory for all practising lawyers, with members having professional indemnity insurance. Ask your lawyer for proof of membership and feel free to double-check with the association if you have any doubts.

Experienced – should have plenty of experience in conveyancing, at least five years (the more, the better), preferably with foreigners.

Independent – last but not least, should represent and protect your interests throughout the transaction. Yours and only yours. Not those of the seller or estate agents.

What does a lawyer do?

In a nutshell, your lawyer will ensure you buy a property with complete peace of mind. Specifically, a lawyer does the following:

- Carries out checks on the property and its owner.
- Finds out if there are any charges or encumbrances on the property.
- Checks outstanding debts for taxes, local council rates and community fees.
- Negotiates the terms of the purchase contract with the seller on your behalf.
- Drafts a purchase contract in your interests and ensures there are no clauses that leave them unprotected.
- If necessary, signs the purchase contract on your behalf.
- Ensures you and the seller comply with all terms of the contract before completion.
- Accompanies you to the notary's office, checks that the title deeds are as agreed, and explains them to you before you sign them.
- Ensures all property taxes and fees (see page 97) are paid after the purchase.
- Sets up direct debits for utilities, local taxes and community fees.

Legal fees can be high (they usually cost 0.5-1% of the purchase price), but they're a drop in the ocean compared to what you're paying for your new home.

It's also true that taking legal advice can make the purchase procedure longer – some checks on the property take time. However, if an extra couple of weeks mean you can buy with peace of mind, the wait will be worth it.

Estate agent (*agente inmobiliario*)

Estate agents handle most sales in Spain and unless you buy privately, you will probably use their services. There are many excellent professionals, but estate agents don't have a good reputation in Spain. However, if you ask for recommendations from people you trust and do your research on the internet, you should end up with a shortlist of the good ones.

It's also worth finding out:

Their qualifications – Spanish estate agents aren't regulated by law, but many are members of professional organisations. They include Colegio de Agentes de la Propiedad Inmobiliaria (API, usually provincial) and Agencia Nacional de Agentes Profesionales Inmobiliarios (ANAPI). These associations have codes of conduct. Ask to see the agent's credentials.

Their track record – choose an agent who has been working for at least five years in the area, preferably longer. An experienced agent will have extensive local knowledge, understand the market and have a good idea of future price trends and their possible consequences.

Their enthusiasm – you're making a substantial investment, so look for an agent who's enthusiastic about finding you the home of your dreams. Make sure their motivation is helping you, not just the money they'll earn in their commission.

What does an agent do?

A good agent does the following:

- Listens to your wish list and searches for properties that tick these boxes.
- Offers advice on different areas and their pros and cons.
- Provides comprehensive information on the properties you're interested in,

TOP TIP

Read the agent's 'About Us' page and ask yourself how you feel when you've finished it. If the page reassures you and inspires confidence, you've probably found an agent you'll like. If it doesn't, cross them off your shortlist.

including videos and live walk-throughs if you can't visit in person.
- Arranges viewings and accompanies you on visits.
- Knows how much room there is for negotiation in the price and helps you and the seller agree on a final figure.
- Facilitates information to your lawyer and respects your need for independent legal advice.
- Helps with aftersales services such as recommending specialists for refurbishment, interior design, garden maintenance etc.

For information on estate agent's fees, see page 97.

Surveyor (*perito* or *arquitecto técnico*)

Much of the information in this section has been generously provided by Campbell Ferguson from Survey Spain (surveyspain.com).

Like independent lawyers, a surveyor will work for you, not the agent and/or the seller. As we all know, sellers tend to give a property a facelift before putting it on the market. And like cosmetic surgery, the facelift might lead to a better look but it does nothing to hide the cracks and damage underneath. That's why in almost all purchases, a survey is a good idea and in most, having a thorough inspection of a property is essential. A survey will let you know exactly what you're buying and how much it'll cost in time and effort to correct any faults and damage.

Like lawyers, surveyors should be trained, registered and experienced. Your chosen professional should:

Trained – have an educational background in architecture, engineering or land economy. In Spain, for example, they have usually studied Ingeniería de la Edificación (construction engineering).

Registered – be registered with the appropriate body, Spanish or international. For example, with the technical architects association (Colegio de Arquitectos Técnicos), usually provincial, or an international association such as RICS.

Experienced – have at least five years' experience of inspecting properties in Spain. If you're buying a rural property, choose a surveyor with a proven track record in this field.

What does a surveyor do?

In essence, a surveyor finds all the potential problems in a home and alerts you to them. More specifically, a surveyor does the following:

- Measures the property and checks the legal and tax descriptions to find out if they're accurate.

- Finds out if there have been unauthorised additions to the property that you may be forced to demolish or have to pay a large fine.

- Alerts you to a problematic property that could be costly to put right.

- Tells you which are the critical problems and which aren't. For example, is a crack in the wall a sign that the foundations are failing or merely due to changes in seasonal temperatures and humidity?

- Looks for damp, examines its causes and presents possible solutions. Damp (rising, coming through or dropping down) is the most common problem found in properties in Spain. The consequences are chilly homes, expensive heating bills and damaged paintwork.

- Examines the property's structure to find out, for example, if cracks are a sign that it is sliding (a common problem in properties built on slopes).

- Offers advice on heating and cooling systems already in place and the best options to install.

- Checks the electrical circuits and if the power supply is sufficient.

- Finds out if the water pressure and hot water supply are sufficient.

- Checks the right of access for cars, wells and electricity, and the outflow from the septic tank, particularly in rural properties.

Architect (*arquitecto*)

If you're starting from scratch and building your own home or carrying out substantial refurbishment, you should consider using the services of an architect.

A professional has the knowledge to turn your vision into reality. They also know their way around Spanish paperwork, how to solve design or construction challenges and how to add investment value to your property.

Choose an architect who:

- Listens to what you want and takes these ideas on board.
- Gives you a clear outline of the design and construction processes.
- Provides a timeline for the entire build.
- Is 100% transparent about costs.

As well as the above, ensure your chosen architect is:

Trained – should have a degree in architecture (one of the most challenging disciplines in Spain).
Registered – must be registered with the provincial Architects Association (Colegio de arquitectos). Membership is compulsory for all practising architects in Spain and members have professional indemnity insurance.
Experienced – should have proven experience in designing homes in the area. Ask to see a portfolio of examples and if possible, visit at least one of their completed properties.

For more information about finding the right architect for you, see page 64.

CMYK ARQUITECTOS   I   621 240 379   I   hallo@cmyk-arq.es   I   www.cmyk-arq.es

Notary (*notario*)

A notary is a public official whose services you use when you complete the purchase. Their role is entirely neutral and they represent the law, not you or the seller. Their job is to draft and witness the title deeds while ensuring that they comply with Spanish law. A notary also:

- Does some (but not all) legal checks such as checking the Property Registry entry and charges on the property. However, it's your lawyer's responsibility to do a thorough legal check on the property and ensure that everything's in order before you sign.
- Confirms the identity of both parties.
- Prepares the final signed deeds.
- Reads the deeds to both parties (ask your lawyer for a translation beforehand so you understand what is being read).
- Witnesses the signature of the deeds.
- Confirms the payment of outstanding amounts on the property price.
- Notifies the Property Registry of your purchase immediately after you sign so that no one else can buy the property for the next 10 days while the registry officially enters you as the new owner.

DID YOU KNOW?

It's the buyer's right to choose which notary you use to sign the title deeds and complete your purchase. If you don't have a preference, your lawyer will select one on your behalf.

Paperwork admin expert (*gestor*)

You may have already experienced Spanish paperwork and know that it's complicated, but the good news is that there are trained professionals in Spain whose job is to take care of all paperwork correctly. They are known as a *gestor* (literally, managers) and unsurprisingly they are very busy!

Most lawyers work with a gestor who does the paperwork, so you probably won't need to find one to do it for you. But if you need a reputable gestor, look for one who:

- Comes recommended by others.
- Speaks your language.
- Is registered with the provincial association (Colegio de Gestores Administrativos) because membership shows that the gestor is qualified to offer the paperwork services.

In a property purchase, a gestor typically does the following:

- Collects the original title deeds from the notary and takes them to the Property Registry to register in your name.
- Ensures that all the relevant taxes and fees are paid in full and on time.
- Sets up direct debits for your utility services and property taxes.

Mortgage advisor (*asesor hipotecario* or *intermediario de crédito hipotecario*)

If you need a mortgage to buy your property, you could visit numerous banks to discuss options and deals yourself, a worthwhile option if you have the time (and speak Spanish). If you don't, then you may want to use the services of a mortgage advisor who:

- Speaks fluent Spanish and your language.
- Is fully qualified to offer mortgage advice. In Spain, this involves passing a series of exams set by the Bank of Spain.
- Is registered with the Bank of Spain as authorised to provide mortgage advice.

A mortgage advisor is someone who:

- Has a thorough knowledge of mortgage law and regulations in Spain.
- Advises on the best type of mortgage for you and your financial circumstances.
- Sources the best mortgage deal for you as quickly as possible.
- Helps with the mortgage paperwork.

For more information on getting a mortgage in Spain, see page 91.

TOP TIP

Choose a mortgage advisor who has access to as many mortgage deals as possible, ideally a 'whole-of-the-market' advisor.

Translator (*traductor*)

If your lawyer (and other chosen professionals) speaks your language well, you'll probably not need someone else to translate the documents, e.g. the purchase contract and title deeds. But if this isn't the case or you need the translation of original documents into Spanish, you will need a translator.

Ask around for recommendations, check credentials and compare prices. If you need a sworn translation (*traducción jurada*) for official purposes, for example, your marriage certificate for a family visa, you must use a translator from the government-approved list.

To find one, go to exteriores.gob.es, go to 'Servicios al ciudadano' and click on traductores. Scroll down the page to LISTA ACTUALIZADA with the latest date (about halfway down) and click on the pdf. Then, look for your language (listed alphabetically so German (*alemán*) is first and English comes under *inglés*) and get in contact with a translator.

Fees for sworn translations are higher than regular translations because of the official nature of the text, which the translator stamps and signs as true and accurate. You pay per word (from €0.12) with a minimum fee of at least €60 per document. The translation of documents in less-common languages such as Norwegian or Hebrew costs more.

GETTING A MORTGAGE IN SPAIN

What's inside this chapter

- General information on mortgages
- How to find the best
- The application process and costs

Mortgages or home loans (*hipoteca*) are available from most Spanish banks and foreign banks, both in Spain and abroad. Loan conditions and amounts advanced depend on your status, the bank and sometimes the type of property you're buying.

In this chapter, we look at the types of mortgages available, how long it takes to get a mortgage and the costs involved.

Much of the information in this chapter has been generously provided by Alison de Cotta from Mortgage Matters Spain (mortgagemattersspain.es).

Interest rates in Spain

The benchmark for mortgage interest rates in Spain is the 12-month Euribor, set by the European Central Bank. Spanish banks take the Euribor as their base rate and add a margin. In February 2016, the 12-month Euribor fell below zero where it has since remained. In January 2021, it dropped to its lowest ever rate at -0.505%. You can check the latest and historic Euribor rates at emmi-benchmarks.eu.

The below-zero base rate makes for cheap mortgages and as a result, buyers are taking out more loans than ever. In July 2021, mortgage approvals went up by 36.8% in the year and the average loan was €136,527.

Types of mortgages available

Unlike other countries such as the UK where there's a wide variety of mortgage options, Spain offers a more limited selection. If you're a non-resident, you have the choice of just two: a fixed loan or a variable rate loan.

DID YOU KNOW?

All mortgages in Spain based on capital repayment and there are no interest-only or buy-to-let loans available.

Fixed-rate loan

A fixed-rate mortgage (*cuota fija*) sets an interest rate that remains unchanged (fixed) for the duration of the mortgage. So, if you take out a loan with a 1.59% fixed interest rate for 20 years (lowest available in October 2021), you will pay this rate for the full 20 years unless you remortgage.

Pros & cons – the biggest benefit is that you know exactly how much your monthly payments will be for the entire mortgage. On the other hand, if mortgage rates go down, you're locked into a higher rate.

Variable-rate loan

The interest rate paid on this type of mortgage (*cuota variable*) depends on the variations in the Euribor. Your bank will review the interest rate, usually once or twice a year, and adjust it depending on the 12-month Euribor rate. For example, in October 2021, the cheapest advertised variable rate was 0.83%.

Pros & cons – a variable rate is advantageous if you want to pay off your mortgage early and benefit from a below-zero Euribor. However, as soon as interest rates go up so do your monthly repayments.

How to find the best mortgage

As with all financial products, it's worth shopping around to source the most advantageous loan for you. You could visit lots of Spanish banks and ask for details or you could use the services of a mortgage advisor (*asesor hipotecario* or *intermediario de creditos inmobiliarios*/ICI). An advisor has agreements with all the main Spanish banks and thorough knowledge of the different products available. Using their services involves a fee, but saves you considerable time and stress.

See page 89 for more information on mortgage advisors.

Who can take out a mortgage

Spanish banks are generally happy to lend to non-residents wishing to buy a second home in Spain. That said, they still need to do extensive affordability and eligibility tests (see below) before they approve your loan.

How much can you borrow?

Spanish banks bear the following criteria in mind:

Affordability

As a rule of thumb, you are not allowed to have a debt-to-income (DTI) ratio higher than 30-35%. For Spanish mortgage purposes, this debt includes outstanding loans in your home country in addition to your new debt in Spain.

Eligibility

Spanish banks generally take into account your age, monthly income and net worth (assets and savings). The same applies to your partner. They also require information on other loans you might have and on your credit record.

Loan-to-value

Loan-to-value (LTV) is the amount of the property price that the bank is prepared to lend. The percentage depends on your residency status and nationality:

- Spanish residents – maximum 80% LTV
- EEA non-residents – maximum 70% LTV
- Non-EEA non-residents – maximum 60% LTV

The application process

In this chapter, we've assumed that you're making life easy for yourself and have contracted the services of a mortgage advisor to source a loan for you. In this case, the process will generally be as follows:

1. The advisor provides information on the type of mortgages available, the process and an estimate of the financial figures involved.
2. You provide the relevant financial information and the advisor assesses your eligibility for a mortgage.
3. The advisor submits the client's documentation to banks with viable mortgage options. Banks usually take around 10 working days to respond.
4. The advisor helps you choose the best offer for your circumstances, sets up a bank account with your selected bank and requests a property valuation.
5. The valuer visits the property and submits a report.
6. The bank issues a binding offer to you to review and sign.
7. The binding offer is sent to a notary and you must answer a short questionnaire to ensure you have fully understood the terms and conditions of the mortgage contract. You then have a 10-day cooling-off period during which you may reject the binding offer.
8. Once the 10 days are over, you complete your purchase at the notary in the presence of the bank and sign the mortgage deeds as part of the property title deeds.

TOP TIP

Make sure you read all the small print in your loan contract, including the terms and conditions. Check you understand everything, particularly the clauses that involve penalties such as the costs of early repayment or the cancellation of the mortgage and what happens if you default on payments. Also find out about the potential costs and terms and conditions for any compulsory bank products associated with the loan such as home or life insurance policies.

How long does the process take?

It typically takes six to eight weeks from the initial mortgage application to the end of the cooling-off period.

How much does it cost to get a mortgage?

Home loans involve various fees. In the past, banks passed almost all of these on to the client, but after recent changes in the law, the client incurs minimal costs, as follows:

You pay

- Valuation fee – from €200
- Mortgage arrangement fee – 1-1.5% of the loan, although not all banks charge for this service.
- Mortgage advisor fee – this varies depending on the complexity of the mortgage, but costs are rarely higher than €1,500.
- Copy of title deeds if required – around €50.

The bank pays

- Stamp duty – 0.4% to 1.5% of the loan depending on the region (see Stamp Duty on page 98 for more information).
- Notary and Property Registry fees relating to the mortgage only. You pay any fees relating to the purchase.
- Paperwork arrangement fees.

TOP TIP

If you're buying with a mortgage, factor the application process into your timeline for purchase.

THE COSTS OF
BUYING PROPERTY

What's inside this chapter

A breakdown of costs involved when you buy a property, from fees and taxes to utility connection charges.

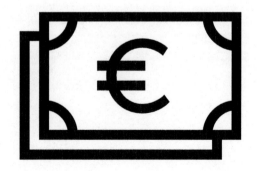

As we've already mentioned, the costs associated with buying property in Spain aren't cheap. On the contrary, they add between 8 and 13% to the purchase price if you buy a resale property. If you purchase a new build, allow for at least 12% on top of the price. You need to factor in these high costs when doing your Maths and working out your budget.

For example, if you're buying a property for €350,000 on the Costa Blanca, you will have to pay around €42,000 in taxes and fees.

This section looks at all the costs incurred for property taxes and services provided by professionals such as notaries and lawyers.

For information on running costs once you've bought the property, see page 118.

Main buying taxes and fees

When you buy a property in Spain, you must pay the following:

- Transfer tax (**resale properties only**) or IVA (Impuesto sobre el Valor Añadido/ IVA, Spanish VAT) and stamp duty (**new-build properties only**)
- Notary fees
- Land Registry fees

You may also need to pay:

- Legal fees
- Estate agent fees
- Surveyor fees
- Mortgage advisor fees
- Mortgage expenses
- Utility connection costs

Transfer tax – resale properties only

If you're buying a resale property (i.e. with at least one previous owner), you must pay transfer tax. Known as Impuesto de Transmisiones Patrimoniales/ IPT, the tax is charged as a percentage of the purchase price and varies from region to region, as the table on the following page shows.

As you see, IPT is considerably more expensive for properties on the Costa Blanca (Comunidad Valenciana, 10%) than in the Balearic Islands (8%) or on the Costa del Sol (Andalusia, 7%). So, for a property with a price of €250,000, you would be liable for transfer tax of €25,000 on the Costa Blanca, €20,000 in Mallorca and €17,500 on the Costa del Sol.

Some regions apply discounts on IPT for first-time young buyers, large families and buyers with disabilities.

Region	Transfer tax
Andalusia	7%
Aragon	8%
Asturias	8%
Balearic Islands	8%
Basque Country	4%
Canary Islands	6.5%
Cantabria	10%
Castilla-la Mancha	9%
Castilla-León	8%
Catalonia	10%
Comunidad Valenciana	10%
Extremadura	8%
Galicia	10%
La Rioja	7%
Madrid (region and city)	6%
Murcia	8%
Navarra	6%

IVA – new-build properties only

The Impuesto sobre el Valor Añadido/ IVA (VAT) is levied at a flat rate of 10% on new properties (i.e. with no previous owners). The rate is the same throughout Spain.

Stamp duty – new-build properties only

If you buy a new-build property, you're also liable for stamp duty. The Impuesto sobre Actos Jurídicos Documentados/AJD has different regional rates, as shown in the table on the following page.

So, for example, if you buy a new home for €250,000 on the Costa Calida (Murcia), Costa del Sol (Andalusia) or in Tenerife (Canary Islands), your purchase taxes (IVA plus AJD) will total:

- Costa Calida - €28,750 (10% + 1.5%)
- Costa del Sol - €28,000 (10% + 1.2%)
- Tenerife - €26,000 (10% + 0.4%)

Region	Stamp duty
Andalusia	1.2%
Aragon	1.5%
Asturias	1.2%
Balearic Islands	1.2%
Basque Country	0.0%
Canary Islands	0.4%
Cantabria	1.5%
Castilla-la Mancha	1.5%
Castilla-León	1.5%
Catalonia	1.5%
Comunidad Valenciana	1.5%
Extremadura	1.5%
Galicia	1.5%
La Rioja	1.0%
Madrid (region and city)	0.7%
Murcia	1.5%
Navarra	0.5%

Notary fees

When you buy property in Spain, you sign the title deeds at a notary's office. Notary fees are regulated by law and are the same throughout Spain. The final costs depend on the price of the property and the length of the title deeds. The more expensive the home and the longer the deeds (for example, if they include information about a mortgage), the more a notary will charge.

For instance, allow around €700 for a property costing €350,000 and €1,000 for a €500,000 home, each bought without a mortgage.

Land Registry fees

Once you have signed the deeds, they are registered in your name at the local Land Registry (Registro de la Propiedad). Registration fees are also regulated by law and, like notary fees, depend on the price of the property.

Budget for between €400 and €1,000.

Legal fees

Fees for a lawyer to carry out the conveyancing for a property usually range from 0.5 to 1.5% of the purchase price. Many lawyers apply a minimum fee of €1,000 for properties priced less than €100,000. Prices are higher if the purchase process is more complicated than usual – for example, if it involves an inheritance or illegal building licence.

Using a lawyer and paying legal fees is optional but highly recommended. Find out more about independent legal advice on page 80.

Estate agent fees

The commission charged by estate agents ranges from 3 to 10% of the selling price. In theory, the vendor pays the fees, but because they are usually included in the price, in practice, the buyer pays them. If you buy the property directly through the owner, you will not be liable for estate agent commission.

Find out more about estate agents on page 82.

Surveyor fees

Surveyors offer a variety of services including property and land inspections and valuations. Their fees depend on the time taken to provide the contracted services. For example, a walk through an apartment giving a verbal report on its condition costs around €300, while a full survey for a large villa costs several thousand euros.

Appointing a surveyor and paying their fees is optional but highly recommended if you're purchasing an older or rural property. Find out more about surveyor services on page 84.

Mortgage advisor fees

Most mortgage advisors charge a set fee for helping you source a mortgage and make the application. It's typically €1,500.

Mortgage expenses

If you're buying with a mortgage, there are certain associated costs. However, thanks to legislation introduced over the last couple of years, banks take on most of these. You may be liable for valuation and opening fees, but some banks no longer charge for these either. See page 95 for the full details.

Utility connection costs

You may have to pay connection or new contract costs for utilities such as electricity, gas and water. The cost will depend on the type of property you buy and whether it's new build or resale.

New-build properties

You usually pay for connection and meter installation when you buy a new home.

Connecting electricity depends on the type of property, the infrastructure already in place and the power supply. For example, expect to pay from €160 for a 3kw supply to a new apartment.

The charge for gas connection depends on the gas supply you need, the infrastructure already in place (new apartment blocks generally have pipes in place and gas companies pay for the first 6m) and a regional charge. For example, connecting gas to a new apartment in Malaga would typically cost from €200.

Water connection charges depend on the size of your meter, which regulates how much water can flow into your home. The larger the meter, the higher the price. For example, connecting the supply to an apartment in Benidorm costs from €100 for a 13mm meter.

Utility connections to properties outside urban areas cost considerably more, particularly if the mains supply is some distance away.

Resale properties

If a utility supply was disconnected when you took possession of the property, you must pay a reconnection charge. Reconnecting electricity to an apartment can cost from €100, gas from €100 and the water supply from €50.

If the utility supplies are still on, all you need to do is change the name in the contract to your name . The company usually does this for free.

TOP TIP

You only need to pay connection or reconnection charges if you buy a new home (i.e. you're the first owner) or the supply has been disconnected in a resale property. Otherwise, you only need to change the contract to your own name. Double-check beforehand!

Final words

As this chapter shows, buying a property in Spain involves a long list of associated taxes and fees. Many of them are unavoidable so when calculating your budget, don't forget to factor in all these costs.

THE PURCHASE PROCEDURE

What's inside this chapter

A step-by-step guide to the legal side of buying property in Spain from finding the property to completion.

The process involved in buying property in Spain may be very different from what you're used to. This chapter looks in detail at the purchase procedure for buying a resale and a new property and the different stages of each process.

Note that although the information in this section is all correct, it's no substitute for professional legal advice. In fact, if you appoint an independent lawyer, they will handle practically all the aspects of the purchase on your behalf to ensure you buy with peace of mind.

The information in this section has been generously provided by Andalusian Lawyers (andalusianlawyers.com).

Before you do anything else

Appoint a lawyer who should be independent, registered and speak your language (see page 80). Ideally, do this before you start looking for a property. When you've found the property you want to buy, get in touch with your lawyer. Do this before you pay anything to anyone (reservation fee or deposit).

Next, you should also do the following:

Get your NIE

For all property transactions (purchase, sale or rental) you need a foreigner's identity number, known as an NIE (*número de identificación de extranjeros* in Spanish). This number identifies you to the Spanish tax authorities and consists of an X or Y followed by 7 or 8 digits and another letter. For example, X-12345678-A.

Note that an NIE has nothing to do with residency in Spain; it's a fiscal and legal document. You are not a resident in Spain unless you have a residence permit.

How to apply for an NIE in person

1. Fill out form EX15 (available online from extranjeros.inclusion.gob.es - go to Modelos Solicitud and click on modelos generales). You must complete the form in Spanish (and in block capitals) so if your Spanish isn't too good, get help.
2. Pay the fees (around €10) at a bank using form Tasa 790-012.
3. Take the EX15, proof of payment, your passport (minimum validity is six months until expiry) plus one photocopy of the relevant pages* to a National Police station with a foreign department. It's also a good idea to take proof of why you need a NIE, for example, a property contract.

(*relevant pages are: EEA nationals, just the pages with your personal details on; non-EEA nationals, all the passport pages even those without a stamp.)

TOP TIP

Buying a property can be an emotional process and often, the heart takes over the head. So, when buying in Spain, don't leave your brain at the airport and don't do anything you wouldn't do in your home country!

Most National Police stations operate an appointment system. To get yours, go to sede.administracionespublicas.gob.es/and proceed as below (using Malaga as the example province):

1. Go to *Provincias disponibles* ➡ Malaga **CLICK** *Aceptar*

2. *Trámites disponibles* ➡ *Policia Certificados y Asignacion NIE* **CLICK** *Aceptar*

3. Read the next page (an overview of getting an NIE in Malaga) **CLICK** *Entrar*

4. **CLICK** passport and enter the number. Then enter your full name **CLICK** *Aceptar*

5. **CLICK** *Solicitar cita* (chose appointment). Select the police station of your choice from the drop down menu and **CLICK** *Siguiente* (next)

6. Enter your phone number and email address **CLICK** *Siguiente*

7. Choose the apppointment date/ time that suits you best **CLICK** *Siguiente*

8. **CLICK** OK, note the appointment. You'll get a reminder by SMS and/or email

How to apply at a Spanish Consulate

You can apply for a NIE at a Spanish Consulate abroad. Check the relevant website for one in your country for details of how to apply and make an appointment.

How to get someone else to apply for you

You can appoint a third party to apply for a NIE on your behalf. This person might be a lawyer, fiscal representative, friend or family member and they must have power of attorney (see below). You need to authorise them to represent you on the EX15 form.

Power of attorney

If you can't be physically present in Spain for the purchase, your lawyer can act on your behalf with a power of attorney (*poder de representación*). Your lawyer will arrange this and you can sign it in Spain at a notary or in your home country at a notary public or a Spanish Consulate. The latter two options take longer and cost more.

Mortgage application

If you need a mortgage, apply for one as soon as possible because approval generally takes 6 to 8 weeks. If you're buying a new build, you may be able to take over the developer's mortgage on the property.

See page 91 for information on getting a mortgage.

The procedure for buying a resale property

 Before you sign any documents or part with any money

Essential checks

There are essential checks that should be taken before you sign any documents or part with any money. Your lawyer will carry out these checks on the property to make sure that you can buy it with legal and financial peace of mind. They include:

- Checking that the property belongs to the seller or that the seller has the legal authority to sell it.

- Checking the Property and Cadastral Registries to ensure the property details are accurate and correctly describe the location, size and type of property. If there's a discrepancy, you may need to hire the services of a surveyor (see page 84).

- Ascertaining whether there are any charges on the property such as encumbrances (e.g. a mortgage) and unpaid debts.

- Ensuring there are no tenants in the property. If there are, your lawyer will ensure you can get vacant possession of the property.

- Making sure there are no pre-emption rights to the property (i.e. someone else such as a tenant has the first right to buy it).

- Verifying that building and occupation licences are correct and legal.

- Ensuring that extensions to the property or additions (e.g. a pool) have planning permission and are registered in the Property Registry.

- Confirming payments to make sure there are no debts with the council, community of owners or utility companies.

- Checking that beachfront properties have approval from the coastal authorities (Jefatura de Costas) and the rights you have. In some coastal areas, property owners have rights of use that must be renewed periodically. In others, the garden might form part of the coastal line and in many cases, it's difficult to obtain permission to restore or rebuild the original building.

Get a survey

It's a good idea to get a qualified surveyor to inspect the property, particularly if you're buying an older and/or rural home. The survey report may affect the price you're prepared to pay or you may need to include a clause for repairs or compensation in the pre-purchase contract. See page 84.

The procedure for buying a resale property

 2   **The pre-purchase contract**

Once your lawyer is satisfied that the property is legal and that any potential problems can be resolved before you purchase, the next step in the process is usually signing a pre-purchase contract and paying a deposit to the seller.

Your lawyer will work in tandem with the seller's lawyer and draw up a pre-purchase contract with all the terms and conditions of the purchase. This includes price, mortgage conditions, the deadline for completion, what's included in the sale etc. Under Spanish law, the contract may contain any clause that both parties agree on.

Once the contents of the contract are agreed, both parties sign it and you pay a deposit, usually 10% of the price. The agreement is now binding. If you decide not to go through with the purchase, you don't usually get your deposit back unless the seller breaks one of the conditions in the contract. If the seller pulls out, they generally have to return your deposit plus the same amount again.

If you are buying the property with any contents (for example, furniture, light fittings, appliances and garden furniture), make sure you give your lawyer a complete list to attach to the contract. Both parties also sign the agreed inventory and it, like the contract, is binding.

TOP TIP

Before you complete the purchase, check that the agreed contents are still in the property. If anything is missing or damaged, ask your lawyer to request that the seller replaces the object or deducts the cost of the item(s) from the final price.

Energy efficiency certificate

All properties sold or rented in Spain require an energy efficiency certificate (*certificado de eficiencia energética*). It describes the property's energy sources and rates its efficiency from A (the best) to G (the worst). It also includes recommendations on how to improve efficiency. It's the seller's responsibility to obtain one before completion and the notary will ask to see it.

The procedure for buying a resale property

 Completion

Completion takes place on or before the date agreed in the pre-purchase contract, usually one to three months after signing the contract. This step takes place at a notary's office, usually chosen by you, the buyer, and involves signing the title deeds, transferring ownership to you and paying the outstanding amount to the seller. If you can't be present, you can give your lawyer power of attorney to buy on your behalf.

The notary draws up the title deeds, which your lawyer checks and if necessary, requests changes. Once your lawyer is satisfied that the deeds are correct, they verbally translate them so you know exactly what the deeds contain (and what you're signing).

The notary also requests the energy efficiency certificate and carries out some basic checks on the property including its entry in the property registry. This is made within four days of completion to ensure that no charges or encumbrances have been placed on the property just before you buy. The notary then verifies your and the seller's identities (passport or ID card) and reads through the deeds in Spanish.

The next step is to sign the deeds and pay the outstanding amount to the seller. You then get the keys to the property that is now yours.

Immediately after signing, the notary sends a copy of the deeds to the Property Registry for provisional registration in your name while the original and final deeds are prepared. This ensures that no one else can buy the property before you are registered as the new owner.

 The property is now yours

Your lawyer organises the registration of the property in your name, the payment of taxes and fees on your behalf and sets up direct debits for utility supplies, the community of owners fees and local taxes.

See page 114 onwards for more information.

The procedure for buying a new-build property

During the last property boom (2004-7), new-build purchases were often fraught with problems. Thousands of buyers in Spain signed title deeds only to find that properties weren't finished, developers went bust or guarantees for payments were worthless. 15 years later, many are still claiming against developers and banks. Some have been successful others are permanently out-of-pocket.

The good news is that tighter legislation and more stringent regulations have made buying off-plan much more secure in Spain. Nowadays, if you use an independent lawyer to act on your behalf, your new-build purchase will have the same security as a resale purchase.

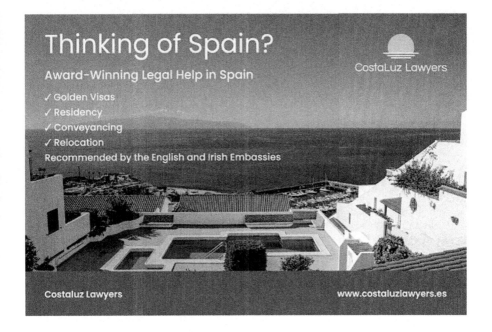

Before you sign any documents or part with any money

Essential checks

There are essential checks that should happen before you sign any documents or part with any money. Your lawyer will carry out these checks on the property to make sure that you can buy it with legal and financial peace of mind. They include:

- Verifying that the developer is a company with a registered name and number.

- Checking that the land belongs to the development company.

- Ensuring that the developer has all the necessary licences and administrative permissions to build the property you want to buy.

- Checking that the developer has a declaration of new construction. If the property is part of a complex and will belong to a community of owners, a declaration of horizontal division is required.

- Checking that you have received the following:

- Plans of the development's location.
- Plans of the property you want to buy.
- Plans of utility supplies.
- A description of the property and the development.
- A list of the type and quality of the materials and finishes in the property.
- A description of the mortgage and its terms and conditions.
- A certificate of energy efficiency.
- If applicable, the regulations and statutes of the Community of Owners.

- Double-checking the developer has a valid guarantee policy in place to safeguard your payments before completion. This policy will ensure your money is refunded if the developer fails to finish the construction work.

The procedure for buying a new-build property

 2   The pre-purchase contract

Once your lawyer is satisfied that the new build is legal and that any potential problems can be resolved before you purchase, the next step is usually to sign a pre-purchase contract and pay a deposit to the developer.

Your lawyer will work in tandem with the developer's lawyer and draw up a pre-purchase contract with all the terms and conditions of the purchase. They include:

- The full price of the property plus IVA (VAT, 10% of the price).
- The stage-payment plan (dates and amounts due).
- Completion date and penalties for late completion.
- Details of the policy guaranteeing your stage payments.
- A clause stating whether you are taking on the developer's mortgage and if so, its conditions.

The contract is usually accompanied by all the relevant plans, details of materials and finishes, community of owner statutes and regulations and the energy efficiency certificate.

Once the contents of the contract are agreed, both parties sign it and you pay a deposit, usually 30-40% of the price. The agreement is now binding. If you decide not to go through with the purchase, you don't usually get your deposit back unless the developer breaks one of the conditions in the contract. If the developer fails to comply with the contract, they must refund all stage payments you have made.

 3   Final checks

Once your property is complete, the developer must allow you to inspect it. If possible, visit it with a specialist (e.g. an architect or surveyor) because you might not notice defects. Take the original list of materials and finishes with you and double-check that they are all present in your new home.

A typical checklist includes:

- **Doors and windows** – do they open and close correctly?
- **Walls and ceilings** – are there any cracks?
- **Paintwork** – are all walls painted to the standard you'd expect?
- **Kitchen** – does it include all the appliances listed in the property description and are they of the stated brand?
- **Bathrooms** – do they include the fittings stated in the property description?
- **Sockets** – are there enough and are they fitted correctly?

The procedure for buying a new-build property

- **Communal facilities** – are they installed and in working order? Check lifts, stairways, gardens and the pool.

Once you have made your list of defects (known as a snag or snagging list), take it to the developer and ask for all of them to be rectified before you buy. Then make a return visit to make sure they have.

> ## TOP TIP
>
> It's much easier to get a developer to fix things before you buy (because they want your money!) but don't worry if this doesn't happen or if you find other defects when you move in. Under Spanish law, you can claim against the developer for minor defects that show within the first year after signing the deeds, within 3 years for defects that affect your everyday living conditions and safety, and within 10 years to claim for major structural faults.

 4   **Completion**

Completion of a new-build purchase takes place on two conditions:

- You are satisfied that the property is as it should be (ie the developer has fixed all the defects in your list).
- The developer has obtained the Licence of First Occupation (licencia de primera ocupación). The local council issues this document to certify that the property complies with all habitation regulations and is fit to live in. This licence is essential and you should never buy without it because you won't be able to contract utility supplies or sell the property in the future.

Completion takes place at a notary public's office, usually chosen by you, the buyer and involves signing the title deeds, transferring ownership to you and paying the outstanding balance to the seller. If you can't be present, you can give your lawyer power of attorney to buy on your behalf.

The notary draws up the title deeds, which your lawyer checks and if necessary, requests changes. Once your lawyer is satisfied the deeds are correct, they verbally translate them so you know exactly what they contain (and what you're signing). Your lawyer also checks the Licence of First Occupation is valid and correct.

The notary also requests the energy efficiency certificate and carries out some basic checks on the property including its entry in the property registry within four days of completion. This check ensures that there are no charges or encumbrances have been placed on the property just before purchase. The notary then verifies your and the seller's identities (passport or ID card) and reads through the deeds in Spanish.

The next step is to sign the deeds and pay the outstanding amount to the developer. You then get the keys to the property that you now own.

Immediately after signing, the notary sends a copy of the deeds to the Property Registry for provisional registration in your name while the original and final deeds are prepared. This ensures that no one else can buy the property before you are registered as the new owner.

 The property is now yours

Your lawyer organises the registration of the property in your name, the payment of taxes and fees on your behalf, arranges connections of utility supplies and sets up direct debits for utility supplies, the community of owners fees and local taxes.

See page 114 onwards for more information about owning a property.

NOW YOU'RE AN OWNER

What's inside this chapter

Information on:
- Moving your belongings
- Running costs
- Refurbishment
- Protecting your home
- Earning income from the property

Congratulations and welcome to your new home! Our final chapter celebrates the fact that you've now bought your property and are ready to start enjoying it. This section is essentially hands-on and looks at the practicalities of owning a property in Spain. We cover topics such as moving your belongings, running costs, home security, insurance, paperwork for residency, refurbishment and finally, how to earn extra income through letting your home.

> ## "Home is the nicest word there is."
>
> LAURA INGALLS WILDER

Moving your belongings

You might have bought a furnished property or are moving into an empty one. Whatever the case, you'll probably be transporting some or all of your things from your home country to Spain.

This section offers advice on choosing a removal company, tips on what to do before you move (including the all-important timing) and after you arrive.

Choosing a removal company

There's plenty of choice, but how do you know which company will offer you the best service for your money? To help you select the right one for you, bear the following in mind:

Get recommendations – ask around for referrals from friends or on expat groups on Facebook, for example. When searching online, read the reviews on the company's Google page and social media profiles. Check the replies to reviews too – considered answers show good customer service.

Choose a company with experience in Spain – and preferably one that makes regular journeys to your chosen location in Spain. This will make your shipment cheaper and possibly quicker.

Check the company's accreditation – as well as good reviews from satisfied customers, find out what accreditation the company has. FAIM and ISO are two international quality standards worth looking out for. Also check to see if the company belongs to an international removal organisation such as FIDI.

> ## TOP TIP
>
> Start planning shipment at least 3 to 4 months before you need your things in Spain.

Get several estimates – at least three will give you a good idea of what your removal will cost. Don't forget to factor in items in your loft/garage/garden if you're taking them with you too. A reputable company will send a representative to your home to give you a detailed and accurate quotation.

Find out about insurance – before committing to a removal company, ask about their insurance cover. Find out precisely what is included (and what isn't). Is it enough to cover damage and/or loss of your things? Consider taking out your own insurance for extra peace of mind.

Use the packing service – moving belongings is always much easier, quicker and less stressful if someone else does the packing for you. Find out if the company offers this service and if they do, take it. The extra cost will far outweigh your time and effort.

Check their tracking service – the best removal companies allow you to track your things in real-time so you know exactly where your things are.

Customs

If you're using the services of a removal company, they should take care of all the paperwork required for importing your belongings into Spain. The rules are as follows:

EU nationals

There are no customs formalities and you can import your things duty-free as long you paid tax for them in the EU or have owned them for at least 6 months. It's a good idea to include an inventory with your belongings (in case of a customs check) and you must attach a copy of your passport.

Non-EU nationals

You can import your belongings duty-free into Spain as long as you have lived outside Spain for at least 12 months (you need a consular certificate to prove it) and have the following paperwork:

- Copy of your passport.
- Copy of residence permit or proof of application for one.
- Certificate of local residence (*empadronamiento*).
- Inventory of your belongings and their approximate value.

You must have used all the imported belongings in your previous home and plan to use them for the same purpose in Spain. You cannot sell or rent out the imported goods for 12 months after entry into Spain.

Note that if you haven't got a residence permit when you import your belongings, you must provide a bank guarantee for the amount determined by customs (up to 60% of the declared value) and obtain your residence permit within 6 months.

Running costs

Of course, once you've bought the property, it's time to maintain it. This section looks at the main running costs and what you can expect to pay. Most of the costs detailed below are best paid for by direct debit (*domiciliación bancaria*). Make sure your account always has enough funds for these payments and also check that your bank is paying them

Utilities

If you're buying a resale property, your lawyer will organise the transfer of the contracts for electricity, gas and water into your name. If you're buying new, your lawyer will organise the connection to the main supplies. For information on the cost of this, see page 100.

Electricity, gas and water

Spain has dozens of companies that supply electricity and gas while water provision tends to be in the hands of the local authorities such as the council or provincial consortium. Electricity and water supplies are already connected in most resale properties and you need to transfer the contract into your name (your lawyers can arrange this for you). Some properties have gas (mainline in modern properties, gas bottles in older properties) for heating water and/or cooking.

Need to know

- The electricity power supply is 220 volts.
- Sockets are two round pin.
- Light bulbs are Edison screw fitting.

TOP TIP

The Spanish Consumers' Organisation (ocu.org) has a helpful comparison tool (in Spanish only). Put in your region, the energy type (electricity or gas), your current supplier and power rating (usually 3.3 or 4.4kW) and then add the details from the latest bill.

Costs

Energy costs rose sharply in 2021 to over a third more than their 2020 price. The charges vary depending on the provider and it's worth shopping around to find a cheaper one (see Top tip above).

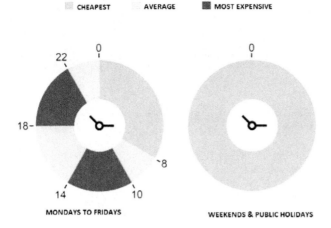

MONDAYS TO FRIDAYS   WEEKENDS & PUBLIC HOLIDAYS

Electricity: In 2021, Spain introduced a three-tier cost for electricity affecting most households. Consumption is most expensive on weekdays 10am to 2pm and 6 to 10pm, with the cheapest rates between midnight and 8am and at weekends.

As well as consumption, your electricity bill also depends on your power rating (the higher it is, the more you pay a month). The final amount includes a small charge for the use of the meter, an electricity tax (around 5% of the total) and VAT (10%).

Some companies allow you to pay a set amount per month (*cuota fija*) irrespective of what you use. Then, at the end of the year, your total consumption is calculated and you pay the outstanding amount or if you paid more than you used, the company refunds you.

Gas: like electricity, gas costs soared in 2021, so shop around for the cheapest provider in your area (see Top tip above). Charges for gas include consumption, a fixed fee for the meter and its usage (charged per day), tax on fossil fuels and VAT (21%).

Water: tariffs vary hugely throughout Spain. For example, in 2021 Murcia had the most expensive water in the country (€26.27 a month for consumption of 9m³) and León the cheapest (€4.83 a month for consumption of 9m³). As well as water usage, you also pay for water treatment and sewerage plus VAT (10%). In most coastal areas and on the islands, there's an additional charge for desalination.

DID YOU KNOW?

Even if you aren't using the property, you will still receive regular bills for energy and water supplies.

Bills

Electricity and gas are billed monthly or every two months, depending on the company and you will receive the bill by post or email (the default option for new contracts). Bills for water are sent monthly, bi-monthly or quarterly, depending on the company.

Telephone and internet

In most cases, you need to contract the service when you buy a property. There's plenty of competition with varying prices and packages.

To help you compare, these 2 websites are useful:

OCU (ocu.org)– Spanish Consumers' Organisation. Put in your region (e.g. Andalucía), select the service(s) you need, choose what you need for each sub-service (e.g. internet speed, mobile data and calls etc). Click on *ver los resultados*.

Rastreator (rastreator.com) – Choose the service you need, select *particulares* (individuals), add your postcode and click on *Avanzar* to see the cheapest deals.

Need to know

- Some deals include minimum contract length (*permanencia* in Spanish).
- Some prices don't include VAT (IVA) or the price of a landline rental.
- Make sure you understand the small print.

For information on the costs involved in setting up utilities, see page 100.

Local council tax

Known as the *Impuesto sobre Bienes Inmuebles* (IBI for short), all properties pay local council taxes for the provision of services such as education, street lighting, local police and cultural and sports amenities.

The amount you pay is based on your property (larger homes pay more) and the council who periodically set rates based on the rateable value plus a coefficient of 1.1% or 2%. As a general rule, rural properties pay less than urban homes. Before you buy, ask your lawyer what the IBI rate is for the property.

Bills: each municipality has different payment plans, although most send out bills for IBI from June to October. Some councils allow you to pay in instalments throughout the year, others offer a discount (e.g. 5% off) for early payment.

Refuse collection tax

Most councils charge separately for refuse collection, but some councils (e.g. Malaga and Barcelona) include it in the local council tax. Prices for this also vary considerably:

Fixed charge – some councils, e.g. Palma de Mallorca, charge an annual fee regardless of the size of the property.

Variable charge – other councils have varied rates that depend on the size of the property, its location and the number of people who live there (usually calculated based on water consumption).

Rates range from €30 to €200 a year.

Community fees

If your property forms part of the community of owners (many do), you have to pay fees for the everyday running and maintenance of the communal areas.

Your fees contribute towards the upkeep and improvement of the common elements. How much you pay depends on the size of your property (the larger the property, the more you pay) and the extent of the facilities (the more there are, the higher the fees). Fees are paid in instalments, e.g. monthly, quarterly or every six months.

Costs may be low, for example, €30 a month for the lift maintenance and cleaning of the entrance hall and corridors or as high as €1,500 a month for apartments with a concierge, security and extensive facilities such as gardens and a pool.

For more information on community of owners, see page 69.

Non-residents property tax

Non-resident property owners in Spain must pay an annual tax (*tributación de los inmuebles urbanos no residentes*).

Cost

What you pay is based on the rateable value of the property (*valor catastral* – included on the IBI receipt) as follows:

- Councils (the minority) that have revised their rateable values within the last 10 years – **1.1% of the rateable value**.

- Councils that haven't revised their rateable values in the last 10 years – **2% of the rateable value**.

You then apply income tax to this figure at 19% if you're resident in the EU, Norway or Iceland or at 24% if you're resident elsewhere (including the UK from the 2021 tax year).

Filing and payment

This tax is payable in the tax year following the previous tax year, so tax for 2022 is paid at any time between 1 January and 31 December 2023.

Who files it

Taxes are always complicated and change every year. So, unless you speak good Spanish, are confident with taxes and keep good records, it's best to use a professional to file this tax for you. Your lawyer will probably offer this service or you can get a tax advisor to do it for you.

WORKING EXAMPLES

If you're Swedish, non-resident and own a property in Marbella (1.1%) with a rateable value of €250,000, you must pay €522.50 a year (€250,000 x 1.1% x 19%).

If you're British, non-resident and own a property in Torrevieja (2%) with a rateable value of €150,000, you must pay €720 a year (€150,000 x 2% x 24%).

Refurbishing your home

Unless you're moving into a fully-modernised home or a new build, the chances are you'll want to carry out some refurbishment work. This section offers general information on how to go about getting permits and finding the best professionals to do the work for you.

Planning permission and building permits

As a general rule, all refurbishment needs permission from the local council. There are two types of licence – one for major works (*obra mayor*) such as building an extension, adding a pool or installing larger windows; and one for minor works (*obra menor*) such as changing a bath for a walk-in shower or refitting your kitchen.

Apply at the planning department at your local council detailing the work and its estimated cost. You then pay a local tax (based on the estimated cost and whether you need to keep a skip in the street) and wait for approval. Some councils are efficient and reply quickly, while others take several weeks. If you don't get an answer within three months of your application, it has automatically been approved.

Major works

If you've bought a property in a dilapidated state that requires extensive restoration, ensure you do the following:

- Before making any firm plans, contact the local council to find out exactly what sort of building work you're permitted to do. Strict planning regulations exist throughout Spain and work carried out without the correct permits risks a heavy fine and/or demolition.

- Employ an architect (see Chapter 3B) or an architectural engineer (*arquitecto técnico*) for advice on the feasibility of the work and how to go about it.

- Apply for the building licence and don't start any work until you have approval.

- Include a contingency fund in your budget, particularly if you're doing major work on an older property.

- Expect the work to take longer and cost more than originally planned.

DID YOU KNOW?

The average cost of refurbishment for a standard home is €350 per m² and €650 per m² for a high-end property. Refurbishment increases the property value by between 20% and 50%.

Finding a builder

Like everywhere else, builders in Spain range from expert artisans to fly-by-night labourers (known as *chapuceros* in Spanish). And as is the case universally, the lowest prices rarely mean the best quality of work.

To find the professionals, ask around for recommendations – the estate agent, lawyer and surveyor may be able to provide some good contacts. When you have got a shortlist, get references from previous customers or, better still, ask to see examples of the builder's completed projects.

Quotations

Get at least two estimates from reputable building companies and make sure they include everything. Find out if the estimates include VAT (they usually don't) and don't forget to factor that into the final price.

Don't be tempted to pay under the table (i.e. without a receipt and paying no VAT) to save money because:

a)   you'll have no guarantee for the work done
b)   and you won't be able to deduct the expense of the work from your capital gains tax when you sell.

Most builders will ask for a deposit to start the work, a percentage halfway through and the final balance on sign-off.

Supervision

If you're having refurbishment done when you're not in the property, hire someone to supervise it for you. The building company may offer this service or you might prefer to use an independent professional such as an architectural engineer (*arquitecto técnico*). Whoever you employ, make sure you provide detailed instructions on exactly what you want done and ask to receive regular updates on progress.

Protecting your home

You've just made a major financial investment in your property so it follows that you should do everything you can to protect it. Measures you can take include home insurance, security and making your home smart.

Home insurance

The information in this section has been generously provided by Liann Cunningham from AXA. If you'd like a no-obligation quote for home insurance, please contact info@guidetomalaga.com.

Numerous companies, including internationally known names, offer insurance (*seguro de hogar*) in Spain providing varying types of cover for the building and its contents.

Building (*continente*) – includes all walls, ceilings, doors, floors, roofs, foundations, built-in wardrobes, windows, gas installations, pipes, water pipes, telecommunications, heating, aircon, shutters and false ceilings.

Contents (*contenido*) – includes furniture, appliances, electrical and electronic items, clothing, furnishings, food, personal items, pets, electric bikes and mobility scooters, jewellery, works of art and rugs. It also covers people living in the house and third parties staying in the property at the time of the incident or damage.

What is partially or not included

Regular policies usually provide 25% cover for personal use items and furniture kept in storage rooms or units. They don't tend to include kitchen units or trees or plants.

Note that you must declare individual items of jewellery worth over €5,000 and single works of art, tapestries and rugs worth over €10,000.

What home insurance covers

The extent of cover varies depending on the insurance company and the policy you take out, but the best insurance policies include the following:

- Material damage (fire, explosion, lightning, electrical surge, water and atmospheric phenomena).
- Additional expenses after the event (e.g. demolition and clean-up, firemen and aesthetic restoration).
- Theft and vandalism.
- Glass breakage.
- Damages caused by forces of nature.
- Water loss up to €500.
- Blockage removal costs regardless of the resulting damages.
- Pipe repair if there are no resulting damages (up to €150).

- Civil liability insurance (usually up to €1,200,000 per accident).
- Private civil liability insurance.
- Civil liability insurance for dog owners.
- Legal protection.

Cost of home insurance

The price depends on the policy you take out and the value of your contents. The following figures give you a general idea of the cost of comprehensive insurance cover:

2-bedroom apartment – from €100 a year.
3-bedroom townhouse– €300-500 a year.
Detached villa with garden and pool – from €500 a year.

Regular policies usually provide 25% cover for personal use items and furniture kept in storage rooms or units. They don't tend to include kitchen units or trees or plants.

Note that you must declare individual items of jewellery worth over €5,000 and single works of art, tapestries and rugs worth over €10,000.

10 tips on choosing the best home insurance policy

As with all insurance policies, it's a good idea to shop around and compare prices. When you're doing that, bear in mind the following:

- The cheapest policy isn't necessarily the best. Read all the small print and if in doubt, choose a reliable, well-known company.

- Make sure you state if you are living full time in the property. If it's your second home or you do holiday lets, prices vary.

- Make sure you have a named agent at the company so that you have someone to speak to personally. They will make your life much easier when you have a claim because they'll take care of it from your initial phone call to final payment.

- When valuing your belongings, make sure you include all of them. If there's a fire or flood, you'll need to replace everything.

- Don't forget to detail jewellery, watches and items valued at over €5,000. Take a photo of each item.

- Check all the exclusions in the policy and double-check that you have sufficient cover.

- Check the limits on your contract to make sure they're high enough. It's best to amend them when you take out the policy and pay the extra than get a shock if you need to claim later.

- If the policy is for a holiday home, check the terms and conditions. They might specify that shutters be left down and the water supply turned off when the property is empty.

- Remember that insurance is for accidental damage, not for wear and tear. Maintaining the property is your job.

- Find out if adding security measures to your home (see next section) such as an alarm reduces the cost of the policy.

Home security

Security is always important in a home and essential if your property will be empty for long periods. The crime rate in Spain is generally low, but burglaries do occur so it's worth doing all you can to make it difficult for thieves to get into your property.

Some ways to help keep your property safe include:

- When you take possession of the property, change the locks on all the entrances – you never know how many people have keys to them. If possible, fit deadlocks with numbered keys that cannot easily be copied.

- If the property has ground-floor windows, make sure they have locks or fit iron grills (*rejas*).

- Put a spy-hole on your front door so you can see who's at the door before you open it.

- Fit an alarm (preferably with a direct connection to the security company). Costs start at around €30 a month.

- Install a smart-home system (see below) that alerts you to the presence of anyone in the property when you're not there.

- Buy a property on a gated complex with 24-hour security or on a development with round-the-clock security.

- Install exterior motion lights in the garden or patio as well as random-timed switches for lights inside the property.

- Never leave anything of real value (financial or sentimental) in your holiday home.

- Employ a house sitter/ someone you trust to check regularly on the property.

- Install smoke and gas detectors.

- Turn off the water and gas when you leave the house for extended periods.

DID YOU KNOW?

Spain has one of the lowest crime rates in the EU. For example, in 2019 (latest available on Eurostat), Spain had 374.65 thefts per 100,000 people compared to 1,235.84 in Germany and 1,352.58 in the Netherlands.

Smart homes

One of the best ways to protect your property, particularly from a distance, is by making it a smart home using the latest technology and your mobile phone. In this section, we look at the advantages of having a smart home and how it can increase your security and peace of mind.

The information in this section has been generously provided by Niki Papdi from Make Me Smart (makemesmart.es).

10 advantages of having a smart home

- It improves safety and security in your home and provides specific solutions for vulnerable people such as the elderly, disabled and children.

- It increases energy efficiency, ultimately saving you money.

- It contributes towards a more sustainable lifestyle.

- It enhances the efficiency of heating and lighting in your home.

- It saves you time because many tasks are automated.

- It gives you control through a single app that you can operate remotely, even when you aren't in the property.

- It offers flexibility and you can always upgrade or add extra functions depending on your needs.

- It's user-friendly and requires no special tech skills or knowledge.

- It increases the value of your property.

- It gives you peace of mind and increased comfort.

How to make your home smart

There are a variety of systems you can put in place in your home and operate via an app on your smart device (phone or tablet). They include:

Smart security features

Intruder alarm – a sensor alerts you via your device when someone tries to enter your home. It can include cameras so you can see in real time what's happening at your front door so you can take action such as calling the police.

Smart lock – this system ensures you are never locked out of your house because instead of a metal key, you unlock the door via a phone app, password or fingerprint. A smart lock also enhances security in your home and allows you to give temporary access to friends, visitors or a delivery person.

Occupancy simulator – this device confuses potential burglars by turning lights on and off and making noises at different times of the day. As a result, it looks as if your property is occupied.

Home features

Smoke, gas and water sensors – they detect leaks instantly and notify you via your app, allowing you to take immediate action to prevent further damage.

Smart light control – this system offers several advantages such as convenience (you can turn lights off via the app without having to get up off the sofa) and energy-saving because lights will automatically turn off when there's no movement in a room. Smart lighting can also adjust colour and brightness depending on natural light conditions or your mood.

Smart temperature control – this feature means you can preset temperatures in your home and turn your heating or cooling system on or off remotely.

Smart power monitor – it monitors your power usage to increase your awareness of how much electricity you're using and can turn appliances on or off to avoid standby consumption.

Smart peace of mind – another feature gives you the chance to control appliances remotely. For example, if you leave the house and can't remember if you turned off the lights, you can check your app and if you did leave them on, turn them off via the app.

The cost of making your home smart

Costs obviously vary depending on the size of your property and how smart you want to make it. As a general idea, expect to pay from:

Basic home automation - from €920 for a 2-bedroom apartment and from €1,250 for a 3-bedroom villa.

Comprehensive smart package - from €1,350 for a 2-bedroom apartment and from €1,850 for a 3-bedroom villa.

Earning income from your home

You might have bought your property with a view to earning money from it as a holiday let or long-term rental. Letting your home for part of the year could help pay for your expenses and even make you a profit. However, paying tenants are never guaranteed, so don't over-estimate the income and never rely on it to pay your mortgage and running costs.

Short-term/ holiday lets

Spain is the world's second most popular holiday destination and as a result, holiday lets are in high demand. However, few places have year-round letting potential and the season varies across the country. Expect 12 to 16 weeks on the Costa Brava, 20 to 24 in the Balearic Islands and 24 to 34 weeks on the Costa Blanca and Costa del Sol. The Canary Islands have the longest season and in the popular destinations, you might get lets for 45 weeks a year.

Rules and regulations

Gone are the days when you could post your property on an online platform, fill it with holidaymakers and pocket the cash. Nowadays, holiday rentals are subject to strict regulations at local and regional level and there are heavy fines for non-compliance.

Also, the Spanish tax authorities are constantly on the look-out for owners who aren't paying tax on the income from holiday lets.

Local level – ensure your community of owners allows holiday lets. If they do, double-check the regulations within the complex to ensure you and your tenants comply with them. Check too that the local council permits holiday lets – in recent years, several (such as Barcelona) have placed a moratorium on them.

Regional level – register your holiday let with the regional authorities. Each region in Spain has different regulations and requirements, although the base system is broadly similar.

For example, there are minimum requirements for space, ventilation and appliances; safety measures must be in place; guests must receive instructions on how to operate appliances, you must supply an emergency contact number and local and tourist information; and the property must have certain equipment such as a first aid kit and fire blanket.

When you successfully register your property, you will receive a licence number, which you must quote on all booking platforms.

Holiday let companies and some estate agents can assist in getting a holiday let licence. Expect to pay from €60 for the service.

Taxation

You are liable for tax on all rental income in Spain whether you're a resident or not. Rates vary depending on your residency status (from 19 to 24%) and you can deduct certain expenses from your tax bill. Use the services of an accountant or tax advisor to make sure you file the correct returns and pay the right amount of tax.

Letting rates

Obviously, rates vary depending on the season, area, type of property and local competition. When you set the rates for your holiday let, research what other owners are charging for similar properties in your area. Don't forget to factor in the cost of utilities (electricity, water, gas and wi-fi) when deciding what to charge.

- High season – Christmas and New Year, Easter week, July and August.
- Mid-season – June and September.
- Low season – the rest of the year.

Property management

If you're letting your property but don't live nearby, it's best to use a property management company to take care of your holiday lets. The most comprehensive services managef everything from bookings to greeting guests via cleaning, maintenance and dealing with complaints. Or you might prefer fewer services and to take on some of the tasks yourself such as managing bookings and payments.

Property management companies usually charge between 20 and 40% of the gross rental income depending on the services provided.

When choosing a management company:

- Ask for references from current clients.
- Make sure you know exactly what services are included.
- Request that the company provides detailed accounts of income and expenses.
- Find out how they market properties and if they vet clients.
- Check the conditions on using the property yourself (some management companies don't allow owners to use it in high season, for example).

Holiday let insurance

When you take out your home insurance policy, make sure you inform the company that you intend to use the property for holiday lets as there's usually a premium. Double-check the small print so you know exactly what's covered.

See also Home Insurance earlier in this chapter.

Long-term rentals

You may have bought the property as a buy-to-let and want to rent it out to long-term tenants. There's currently high demand for rentals in cities and large towns and you'll also find plenty of interest in resorts areas in the winter months.

Rental contracts

Bear in mind that Spanish law generally favours tenants over landlords, but both parties have a series of obligations. The contract must set out the basics and you can agree on other conditions to be included as well.

Length of rental – tenants may stay in the rental for a minimum of 5 years. They only have to leave the property before the 5 years if you, the landlord, need it for a close relative (spouse, child or parent) to live in. However, you can only apply this rule after a minimum of 1 year of tenancy and you must give your tenant 2 months' notice. This option must be clearly stated in the contract.

Extending rentals – if after 5 years you don't want the tenants to remain in the property, you must give them 4 months' notice before the contract expires. Otherwise, the contact is extended by annual periods for up to 3 more years.

Paying rent – tenants usually pay rent between the 1st and 5th of each calendar month.

Deposits – your tenants must pay a minimum of 1 month's rent and maximum of 2.

Giving notice – your tenants must stay for a minimum of 6 months in the property and give you 30 days' notice when they wish to leave.

Rent rises – during the 5 years' rental, you may increase your rent every year by the official rate of inflation (IPC in Spanish and published every month by the government). Both parties must agree this and include the agreement in the contract. This increase only applies to the 5-year minimum rental period. When this comes to an end, both parties must agree a new rental rate.

Payment of expenses – as a general rule, you pay taxes and fees including community charges and tenants pay for utilities and refuse collection tax (if there is one). However, both parties can freely agree on who pays for what, but make sure the contract states exactly who is responsible for each expense.

Maintenance of the property – under Spanish law, you must carry out all maintenance to keep the property habitable except when the tenant causes the damage. In practice, this means you're responsible for maintaining and repairing pipes, walls, ceilings and floors and the tenant is responsible for repairs of blinds, locks, paint, taps and toilets.

Improvements to the property – if you invest in improvements, you can charge the tenants for these in monthly instalments but only after the minimum stay period of 5 years and for no more than 20% of the regular monthly rent. Again, this is open to negotiation. The law states that both parties can freely agree that the improvements made during the first 5 years can be charged to the tenant and without the limit of 20% of the rent. But this must be a clear agreement and incorporated into the contract.

Work on the property – if your tenants want to make any improvements to the property, however small, they need written permission from you. If they carry out work without it, you can cancel the contract and oblige the tenants to pay for everything to be returned to its original state.

Sub-letting and alternative use of the property – unless the contract says otherwise, your tenants cannot sublet the property or use it for anything other than for their residence (working from home is obviously an exception to this).
Inventories – prepare a full inventory of all the contents in the property to attach to the contract. Both parties must sign it.

Checking damage – tenants generally have 30 days after they move in to check for damage, things that don't work etc and report it to you. You are obliged to repair the damage and faults.

TOP TIP

You can get a general idea of rental rates in an area on property portals such as Idealista (https://www.idealista.com/en/maps/). Choose your region, province, municipality and, if applicable, district and click on consult report. You then see the average asking price per m² for the previous month.

Rental rates

What you can charge monthly for your property will depend on its size, location and local competition. As well as checking online (see Top Tip below), it's also worth checking rental advertisements to get a more detailed picture of what other landlords are charging for similar properties.

Rental insurance

You can take out a policy to cover your expenses (and monthly rent) if your tenants don't pay and/or refuse to leave the property. Many insurance companies offer this cover, known as *seguro de garantía de alquiler*, and prices depend on the rental rate and range from 3% to 5%. For example, if the monthly rent is €700, the annual policy will cost from €252 to €420.

Note that policies come with specific conditions such as the tenant must have a clean credit record; an employment contract; and the rental rate is less than 45% of the tenant's income.

House insurance

You should take out cover for the building and the contents included. Make it clear to the company that you let the property and inform your tenants that your insurance policy excludes their belongings. Some insurance companies such as AXA cover damage caused by the tenants in the policy.

Residency paperwork

If you're buying a property in Spain with the view to moving there permanently, you'll need a residence permit. In this section, we take a look at the main options.

The paperwork required, procedure and timescale depend on whether you're an EEA national (EU countries plus Iceland, Liechtenstein, Norway and Switzerland) or a non-EEA national (UK included from 1 January 2021).

Note that the information included in this section is correct as of January 2021. Regulations on permits and paperwork requirements can change so always check with official government sources as well. You can find all the information, rules and downloadable forms (in Spanish) on the Immigration Portal.

Due to the complexity of residence permits (particularly for non-EEA nationals), we recommend that you use professional services to get yours. You will save considerable time and stress and ensure that you present the correct paperwork from day one.

DID YOU KNOW?

Guide to Malaga also publishes two relocation guides:
Your Guide to Moving to the Costa del Sol
Your Guide to Moving to the Costa Blanca
They contain all the information you need for a smooth and stress-free move to these popular coasts in Spain. You can also sign up for quarterly updates so you always have the correct information at your fingertips. Go to guidetomalaga.com/shop, click on the ebook of your choice and get 25% off your copy when you use the discount code WEB at the checkout.

EEA nationals

As a member of an EEA country*, you have the right to live and work in Spain without a visa. If you plan to stay in Spain for longer than 3 months, however, you need to become resident. You must apply for a residence certificate (*certificado de residencia*) within 3 months of your arrival in Spain.

Must-have paperwork

- Completed form EX-18.
- Your passport plus copy.
- Proof you have paid the fee (€12 in 2021).

Plus the following (original and copy) depending on your status:

Employee – employment contract duly registered with the Spanish Employment Department (SEPE).

Self-employed – proof of self-employment (e.g. certificate of signing up to social security, inscription in Business Registry (Registro Mercantil)).

Not working – proof of healthcare cover (state or private) and proof of sufficient funds (income of over €403 a month in 2021).

Student – proof of registration in education centre, proof of healthcare cover and proof of sufficient funds.

Family dependents (your spouse, children or parents) – proof of relationship with you, proof of economic dependence on you, proof that you are working or have healthcare cover for the dependent and sufficient funds. Family dependents need to complete form EX-19 downloadable here.

*EEA countries are: the 26 EU members (Austria, Belgium, Bulgaria, Croatia, Cyprus, Czech Republic, Denmark, Estonia, Finland, France, Germany, Greece, Hungary, Ireland, Italy, Latvia, Lithuania, Luxembourg, Malta, Netherlands, Poland, Portugal, Romania, Slovakia, Slovenia, Spain and Sweden) plus Iceland, Liechtenstein, Norway and Switzerland.

EEA nationals - application process

Step 1

Book an appointment online and follow the steps below (example given for Alicante province).

1. Go to *Provincias disponibles* ➜ Alicante **CLICK** *Aceptar*

2. **CLICK** *Policia- certificado de registro de ciudadano de la UE* and *Aceptar*

3. **CLICK** *Aceptar* again

4. Fill in your NIE or passport number (with no spaces or dashes) plus name and surname. **CLICK** *Aceptar*

5. **CLICK** *Solicitar cita* (chose appointment). Select the police station of your choice from the drop down menu and **CLICK** *Siguiente* (next)

6. Enter your phone number and email address **CLICK** *Siguiente*. ✓ the captcha box.

7. Choose the apppointment date/ time that suits you best. You'll get a reminder by SMS or email

Step 2

Go to your appointment (arrive 30 minutes early as there is often a queue to get in). The member of staff will check your documentation and if it is correct, issue you with your residence certificate. This states your name, nationality, address, NIE and date of registration.

Non- EEA nationals

If you're a third-country national (i.e. not from the EEA), your first step is to apply for a visa at a Spanish consulate in your home country. There are various visa types including:

Non-lucrative visa

This is is an option for a retiree or someone who does not plan to work in Spain (you cannot work for a Spanish company or set up a company (or a branch of a one) in Spain under the terms of this visa).

Must-have paperwork

- Completed form EX-01.

- Proof you have at least €26,000 in a bank account in your name (a bank statement for the last six months will suffice).

- Private medical insurance. Note that you must take out the policy with a Spanish insurance company for a minimum of one year. The policy must not include any form of copayment.

- Proof that you have accommodation or the means to pay for it.

- Proof that you have no criminal record in Spain or your home country.

Note that all documents (except your passport) must be translated into Spanish and where necessary, be authenticated with the Hague Apostille.

Investment visa

To qualify for this visa (also known as the Golden Visa), you must invest in property worth at least €500,000 or Spanish government bonds worth at least €2 million or shares in Spanish companies worth at least €1 million. This visa offers a residence permit for you and your dependents and you don't have to live in Spain for 183 days a year.

Must-have paperwork

- Completed form.
- Private medical insurance. Note that you must take out the policy with a Spanish insurance company for a minimum of one year.
- Proof of sufficient funds to support yourself.
- Proof of the investment (e.g. public debt certificate from the Bank of Spain, certificate of investment funds, bank certificate for deposit, property title deeds…).

Visa to work for someone else

You must have a work visa in place before you arrive. Do this in conjunction with your employer. Generally speaking, your application will be successful if your job has a shortage of qualified applicants, it was advertised locally with no suitable EEA applicants and you have the appropriate professional qualifications.

Must-have paperwork

Once your employer has started the application for your work visa, you should complete your application within 1 month at the Spanish embassy in your home country. You'll need to present:

- Completed form EX-03.
- Certified copy of your employment contract.
- Your passport (at least 4 months' validity).
- Medical certificate.
- Proof of a clean criminal record for the last 5 years.

Visa to work as self-employed

If you plan to set up your own business in Spain, you will need to provide a comprehensive business plan plus proof that you have the financial backing to establish it.

Must-have paperwork

- Completed form EX-07.
- Proof that you have the qualifications and/or experience for your business.
- Proof that you have sufficient funds or financial backing.
- A business plan that includes the amount of investment, expected returns and if applicable, the number of jobs you plan to create.
- Proof of funds to support yourself (as well as your business expenses).
- If you have premises (or plan to open them), proof that you have started proceedings to secure these and proof of the stage the proceedings are at.

Application process

1. Submit your application together with the required paperwork and appropriate fee to a Spanish Consulate in your home country. Wait for approval (this can take up to 3 months).
2. When you receive approval, go in person to the Consulate with your passport to have the visa stamped in it.
3. Move to Spain (you must usually do this within 3 months of getting the visa).
4. Within 1 to 3 months (depending on the type of visa), pay the fee online (€15.92 in 2021) via this link and book an appointment for your TIE (residence permit).

About Joanna Styles

Joanna is a freelance writer and author based in Malaga, which she sees as just about the perfect place to live. Joanna first arrived on the Costa del Sol in 1989 ready to start a new life with her husband.

Her writing journey began with Survival Books updating 'bibles' such as *Buying a Home in Spain* (a best-selling publication between 1997 and 2010) and writing *Culture Wise Spain* and *Costa del Sol Lifeline*, among others (now all sadly out of print).

She then specialised in writing about property investment, particularly in Spain, the US and South America. Since 1998, Joanna has authored dozens of property reports, compiled tens of brochures about buying property and written numerous articles for publications such as *A Place in the Sun*. She also regularly translates property reports for Tinsa, Spain's largest valuation company. You can find out more about Joanna's copywriting on her website (joannastyles.com).

Away from the keyboard, Joanna has first-hand experience in property too. In her more than 30 years in Spain, she has bought and sold several properties and let and rented homes. Her husband is a Spanish lawyer who specialises in conveyancing, and he has shared his knowledge and experience with her over many a dinner table.

Joanna is also the creator and CEO of Guide to Malaga (guidetomalaga.com), the leading website for information in English on Malaga city that welcomes around 30,000 visitors a month. She has also written two relocation guides (Costa Blanca and Costa del Sol) and a travel guide to Malaga, and compiled a Malaga cookbook. All are available from the Guide to Malaga ebook store (guidetomalaga.com/shop).

Acknowledgements

This book would not have been possible without the help and support of many people. For their helpful input and answering many questions (and then more questions!), I'd like to thank the experts: Jose María Sánchez, Alejandro Jiménez, Campbell Ferguson, Liann Cunningham, Alison Decotta and Niki Papdi.

In the design department, my thanks go to Julia Sánchez Styles, one of my talented daughters who has an amazing design eye. She created the cover and maps. I'm most grateful to Elizabeth Ballantyne for proofing and suggesting ways to improve the book. Thanks also to Sandra Pillock for the final edits.

And lastly, I'd like to say thank you to Spain, specifically Malaga and the Costa del Sol for welcoming me and making me feel so at home.

Copyright notice

Printed in Great Britain
by Amazon

83477737R00088